AMERICAN RAILROADS

THE CASE FOR NATIONALIZATION

AMERICAN RAILROADS

THE CASE FOR NATIONALIZATION

DICK ROBERTS

PATHFINDER PRESS, NEW YORK

Pathfinder Press
410 West Street, New York, NY 10014

To Evelyn Reed

About the Author

Dick Roberts is a staff writer for the *Militant,* the socialist newsweekly, and a former editor of the *International Socialist Review.* He is the author of *Capitalism in Crisis,* a Marxist analysis of the 1974-75 recession.

Contents

Introduction

Railroads are a public necessity.

They are essential to millions of commuters who ride them to and from work. Hundreds of factories across the country receive vital supplies and ship finished products by rail. If the branch lines to these factories were closed, many would have to shut down. Much of agriculture is also dependent on rail transportation.

Yet today the deterioration of the railroads is a striking aspect of the crisis facing American society in the 1980s. A vast and useful social resource is literally being run into the ground.

The urgent need to expand passenger service was dramatically shown during the national gasoline shortage in spring 1979. Gas lines grew in many states, and filling stations were closed most weekends. Millions of people wanted to take trains, but Amtrak proved utterly incapable of handling this demand. In fact, at that very moment, the Carter administration was pressing in Congress for a *43 percent reduction* in passenger mileage. Amtrak ran advertisements in a number of cities: "Don't call us, we can't answer."

The improvement of long-distance passenger service is not the only need. Quiet, clean, and inexpensive electrical rail transportation could go a long way toward relieving the congestion and pollution in major cities. Despite this, efficient mass transportation is placed at the bottom of the list of priorities by Democratic and Republican politicians alike.

Railroads are more fuel efficient than trucks for long-distance haulage, and with added investment and research the railroads could become even more fuel efficient— especially if the roadbeds were upgraded. But the sugges-

9

tion of such changes makes the owners of railroads wheeze and fumble.

A recent issue of the railroad industry's magazine *Railway Age* declared, "The industry as a whole lacks funds for energy research." The article goes on to quote a railroad official: "If we had the money, if we didn't have to live from hand to mouth, we'd probably have a pretty good energy program by now."

While shrinking back from needed efforts to improve transportation in this country, the railroads have quietly launched their own reorganization program. One of their aims is to drastically reduce the size of the railway labor force and to greatly intensify the work that the remaining workers have to do. This is an antilabor campaign that threatens the standard of living—and the lives—of rail workers across the country.

On certain railroads, such as the Milwaukee Road and the Rock Island, this attack has taken the form of attempting to liquidate these bankrupt companies in such a way that thousands of workers will lose their jobs with little or no compensation.

Reductions in crew size—called *crew consist*—are spreading from railroad to railroad. This began on the Milwaukee Road and Conrail in 1978, under the excuse that these companies were bankrupt. But in 1979 the Burlington Northern announced it also intended to reduce crews. It offered no excuse, despite the fact that the BN is one of the most powerful and profitable railroad companies in the country.

Stepped-up harassment of railroad workers doesn't end with crew reductions. On the Soo Line in Minneapolis in the bitter-cold winter of 1978-79, "you couldn't lay off. Everyone was working twelve hours day after day," workers said.

Railroad workers are also forced to work under increasingly dangerous conditions which affect the communities along the right-of-way. Liquified propane explosions and the release of deadly anhydrous ammonia gas have brought tragedy to several small southern towns along the railroads.

The railroads also carry most radioactive waste materials. Spent nuclear fuel is shipped by train, including all high-level waste from nuclear weapons production. Often this radioactive material is not even labeled! Washington uses the excuse of "military security," but the end result is to hide hazardous cargo from railroad workers and the towns the railroads go through.

In face of mounting attacks on railroad labor, there are opening skirmishes of resistance. In Minneapolis, five United Transportation Union (UTU) locals and a number of leaders of other rail unions sponsored a protest meeting in June 1978 to present the arguments of those who would be most affected by the Milwaukee Road bankruptcy. Similar meetings were held in Chicago and Milwaukee. A petition campaign to demand that the Milwaukee Road be nationalized was launched in Minneapolis.

A dramatic protest against Conrail took place in early 1979 in the Youngstown, Ohio, and Pittsburgh yards. It was in response to the company's attempt to pull three conductors out of service for exercising their right of early quit-time—a right won by railroad workers decades ago. These Conrail workers had been subject to crew reductions and other forms of harassment. They were fed up, and when the conductors were pulled out in Youngstown, the workers shut down the yard the next day.

All of the approximately five hundred workers in the Youngstown yard respected the protest—from the clerks to the engineers. Many got out in roving buses to spread the word to other yards. Within three days they had shut down the huge Conway yard near Pittsburgh, one of the largest yards in the country, with more than 5,000 workers. As in Youngstown, the Pittsburgh protest was 100 percent solid, involving all of the crafts. And in another two days the protest was spreading throughout the region.

The pressure on Conrail headquarters in Philadelphia was intense. On the sixth day of the protest Philadelphia gave in. The conductors were reinstated.

Such militant struggles have so far remained isolated. They aren't reported in the press and most railroad workers probably do not realize the extent of the willingness to fight back and the potential that exists for resisting the carriers.

"We sometimes don't know what's taking place in the next terminal, let alone nationally," is a frequent complaint.

Keeping railroad workers in the dark about the national

attack on them and the resistance when it takes place is part of the strategy of the companies. They want to take advantage of the fact that there are a number of different railroad lines, as well as different unions on the railroad, to isolate and confine the fight-back. This also helps the long-standing propaganda campaign addressed to the general public that "railroad workers have it so good" and that "featherbedding" by the railroad workers is one of the reasons the railroads are in decline.

For the basic explanation of the state of American railroads, however, we must look elsewhere. It lies in the private ownership of railroads and in the profit drive that powers every move the railroad companies take. To a certain extent the "decline" of the railroads is itself a myth. Freight-hauling is on a sharp increase in the American economy today. Using "piggyback" cars, giant hoppers, triple-deck auto carriers, and the unit train, the big railroads are trying to reorganize their lines into a few freight-hauling giants. Eliminating branch lines and smaller companies, liquidating passenger traffic, reducing the railway labor force, and speeding up the remaining jobs are all part of this private-profit drive.

This book argues that reorganization of the railroads in this country is indeed an imperative necessity. But the railroads should be reorganized according to the needs of the working people, farmers, and small businesses the railroads are supposed to serve. They should not be run for private profit. They should be nationalized and run for the benefit of society.

In many ways the railroads are a microcosm of the economic interests that dominate capitalist America. For decades the railroads were the biggest and most powerful capitalist industry. Their owners—the Vanderbilts, Harrimans, and others—controlled state and federal legislatures and strutted through the courts of Europe. The history of the rise and decline of this capitalist empire and the class forces it has thrust into motion sheds light on the underlying causes of America's economic crisis today.

In truth the railroads should have been nationalized a long time ago. Today it is an urgent necessity in the fight against deteriorating social conditions in the United States.

The New York Central

U.S. railroads began and remain privately owned. As such, they have always been the target of extensive financial manipulation. In the second half of the nineteenth century, the rail industry was the number-one money-maker in the American economy. Until late in the 1800s railroad securities were almost the only ones listed on the New York Stock Exchange. Many ruling-class fortunes were built in rail.

The wealthy businessmen who own the industry are not now and never were concerned with the conditions of railroad cars, stations, or tracks. Least of all are they concerned about the conditions of railroad workers. Their entire preoccupation is with profits, with stocks and bonds.

To trace the roots of the crisis of the railroads today, we must first concentrate on the *finances* of the rail industry.

An eloquent passage in Gustavus Myers's *History of the Great American Fortunes* points in the right direction. "Behold, in imagination at least," wrote Myers, "this mass of stocks and bonds.

"Heaps of paper they seem; dead, inorganic things. A second's blaze will consume any one of them, a few strokes of the finger tear it into shapeless ribbons. Yet under the institution of law, as it exists, these pieces of paper are endowed with a terrible power of life and death that even enthroned kings do not possess. Those dainty prints with their scrolls and numerals and inscriptions are binding titles to the absolute ownership of a large part of the resources created by the labors of entire peoples."

Myers wrote this in 1907 about the Vanderbilt fortune, which grew from Vanderbilt's control of the New York Central railroad. It has lost none of its force more than seventy years later.

From the earliest days, railroad corporations grew out of

13

land grabs by businessmen and politicians, and financial manipulations that saw the mergers of dozens of smaller firms.

In *To Hell in a Day Coach*—one of the best books about American railroads, written in 1968—Peter Lyon notes:

"Long before the first ten thousand miles of track had been laid down in the United States—which is to say, before 1850—the policy of railroad management in respect of the public interest had been set and had hardened: it was to ignore the public interest, dismiss it, sweep it under the rug, and carry on."

Lyon continues, "The Baltimore & Ohio Railroad Company was given, between 1827 and 1850, thirteen million dollars of taxpayers' money by the state of Maryland and the cities of Baltimore and Wheeling, West Virginia; it was also given, tax free, some choice real estate. Again: a committee of the New York state legislature would later reckon that the state and various cities and towns had given New York railroad corporations, among other goodies, $40,039,496.82. . . ."

The history of the New York Central and of the Vanderbilt financial empire goes to the heart of the matter.

The New York Central was founded in 1853 as an amalgam of ten railroad lines running westward from Albany to Buffalo. "Throughout the 1840s," according to Lyon, "there were anguished outcries against [these] railroad companies from scores of citizens, protesting high and discriminatory freight rates, poor passenger service, filthy accommodations, watered stock and other financial monkeyshines, a regrettable trend toward monopoly, and the policy of giving free passes to politicians, favored shippers, and newspaper editors."

In order to put together such monopolies, the railroads bought off entire state and, later, federal legislatures. "Edwin D. Worcester, the treasurer of the New York Central, later acknowledged that the company had spent, from 1853 to 1867, more than a half-million dollars to buy laws at Albany," Lyon says.

When the New York Central was founded, it was capitalized at more than $23 million—an enormous sum at that time. This was almost half the size of the 1853 federal budget.

Cornelius Vanderbilt took over the New York Central

Consuelo Vanderbilt, Duchess of Marlborough, at the corona-
tion of Edward VII. Her marriage to the Duke of Marlborough
in 1895 was arranged by her father, William K. Vanderbilt, who
set aside a $2.5 million trust fund for the duke, in the form of
50,000 shares of railroad stock. Millions more were spent on
wedding gifts and mansions for the couple.

and made it into an even more gigantic monopoly in the
1860s.

The "Commodore" had earlier distinguished himself as a
shipowner. During the Civil War, Vanderbilt sold the
government a fleet of rotten ships. They were barely
navigable on rivers and lakes, let alone on the sea, where
they were supposed to ship troops. It was from the vast
profits from this and other swindles to bilk the government
into subsidizing his ships that Vanderbilt got the capital
he then poured into the rails.

First Vanderbilt took over two parallel rail lines from
New York to Albany—the New York and Harlem Railroad
and the New York and Hudson River Railroad.

New York subway riders may be interested to know—
and in other cities the histories are little different—that in
1832 the New York and Harlem had received a franchise
from the city government for exclusive use of Fourth
Avenue north of Twenty-third Street (the area today of
Grand Central Station, the Pan Am building, and other
vastly expensive midtown real estate, to say nothing of the
Lexington Avenue subway below).

According to Myers's *History of the Great American
Fortunes,* "Vanderbilt not only caused the Legislature in
1872 to pass an act saddling one-half of the expense of
depressing the tracks on the city [making them into
subways—D.R.], but caused the act to be so adroitly
worded as to make the franchise perpetual."

Also, in 1863, Vanderbilt "bribed the New York City
Common Council to give the New York and Harlem
Railroad a perpetual franchise for a street railway on
Broadway from the Battery to Union Square" (right
through the Wall Street area, financial center of Manhat-
tan then and now).

In 1865 Vanderbilt stopped shipping freight from Albany to New York. This cut the throat of the old New York
Central, which could only bring goods from western New
York State to Albany, but not to New York City. Vanderbilt succeeded in forcing the firm to sell out to him, merged
his two other railroads into it, and thus founded one of the
most powerful trusts in U.S. history.

Myers's description of the process of railroad financial
manipulation cannot be bettered: "Often the physical
layout of the railroads—the road-beds, rails and cars—

were deliberately allowed to deteriorate in order that the manipulators might be able to lower the value and efficiency of the road, and thus depress the value of the stock. Thus, for instance, Vanderbilt, aiming to get control of a railroad at a low price, might very well have confederates among some of the directors or officials of that railroad who would resist or slyly thwart every attempt at improvement, and so scheme that the profits would constantly go down. . . .

"The changing combinations of railroad capitalists were too absorbed in the process of gambling in the stock market to have any direct concern for management. It was nothing to them that this neglect caused frequent and heartrending disasters; they were not held criminally responsible for the loss of life. In fact, railroad wrecks often served their purpose in beating down the price of stocks. Incredible as this statement may seem, it is abundantly proved by the facts."

There is considerable evidence that precisely the kind of deliberate running down of a railroad Myers describes was carried out on the Milwaukee Road—not in the 1870s . . . but *in the 1970s.*

The Railroads Push West

From their inception American railroad companies were driven by a greed for profits perhaps unequaled in any other industry. Throughout the nineteenth century, nowhere else was there so much money for the taking. And that attracted not only the leading financiers of the day but also the politicians—from lowly state legislators right on up to the pinnacles of power in Washington, D.C.

Abraham Lincoln's first major legal case was a railroad case in Rock Island, Illinois, in 1857. Lincoln represented the owners of the Farnam Railroad Bridge Company. They charged that some bargemen had blown away the first railroad bridge across the Mississippi. Lincoln won the case.

That rebuilt bridge was a first step in the race of the railroads across the West. Following the Civil War, that race would capture the imagination of Americans for the next three decades.

The story is wonderfully told in a book by Dee Brown, *Hear That Lonesome Whistle Blow*, published in 1977. Brown previously wrote *Bury My Heart at Wounded Knee*. Clearly his interest and support to Native Americans drew Brown into the study of railroads—and he tells us much that we need to know about the history of this industry.

For one thing, the railroads took land away from the Indians. In fact, Lieutenant-Colonel George Armstrong Custer's first expedition against Sitting Bull was to provide military support to a railroad surveying party for the Northern Pacific Railroad in 1873. Sitting Bull's revenge along the Little Bighorn, three years later, is more well known!

In that decade, Brown writes, "an army of hide hunters had invaded the West to slay five million buffalo, almost bringing that native animal to extinction.

"During that same decade, regiments of blue-coated cavalrymen had rounded up thousands of native Americans who were left helpless because of the slaughter of their basic source of food, shelter, and clothing. . . .

"Whenever the Northern Pacific's westward point came to Indian land, a signal went back to Washington, and there the bureaucrats would set a paperwork ritual into motion. Acting in silent collusion, the Office of Indian Affairs, the Secretary of the Interior, the Congress, and the President of the United States arranged for a hasty extinguishment of tribal titles to the land."

To build the railroads, the companies hired armies of the cheapest-paid, largely immigrant labor. Brown notes that the California-based Central Pacific "employed virtually every able-bodied Chinese in California."

These Chinese workers built the steep grades, trestles, and tunnels of the Central Pacific across the Sierras. "For several months during 1867 [there were] eight thousand Chinese tunnelers working in around-the-clock shifts seven days a week." Some five hundred to one thousand died in the effort, Brown estimates.

Another railroad, hurrying across the West from eastern Texas, was the Texas & Pacific. According to Brown, the Texas & Pacific used "Negro prisoners rented from the state of Texas for a few cents a day."

All of this was made possible by Washington's enormous giveaways of land west of the Mississippi. We meet Abraham Lincoln a few more times.

"On July 1, 1862, the day that his Army of the Potomac began retreating in Virginia after the Battle of Malvern Hill," writes Brown, "President Lincoln signed the act, creating the Union Pacific Railroad Company." This act granted the Union Pacific both federal funds and land westward from Iowa. The same act gave the Central Pacific the land from the Pacific Coast to the eastern boundary of California.

On March 3, 1863, Lincoln signed over 2,928,928 acres of Kansas to the Atchison, Topeka & Santa Fe. The charter to the Northern Pacific Railroad Company granted it 25,600 acres per mile from Lake Superior to the Puget Sound.

The Union Pacific–Central Pacific land grant was enlarged in 1864 to give the railroad 12,800 acres of land per mile across the West. Further it granted "all iron and coal deposits under the land to the railroad, and permitted it to sell first-mortgage bonds to the public."

This grand steal was engineered by Union Pacific financier Thomas Durant and Collis Huntington of the Central Pacific. Durant "took $437,000 of Union Pacific funds to Washington for lobbying expenses. . . .

"He also spent a great deal more than that distributing Union Pacific stock to congressmen in exchange for their votes. Even by present-day standards of governmental venality, the methods used by Durant and Huntington were exceptionally crude," Brown adds. Ultimately the Union Pacific got "19,000 square miles, a domain larger than the states of Massachusetts, Rhode Island, and Vermont combined."

But this was only the beginning. Much more was to come, from President Ulysses S. Grant and his successors. Finally, 155 million acres had been given to the railroads, "more than one fourth of the Louisiana Purchase, one ninth of what was then the nation's entire land area."

There is a rule of economics almost as old as class society: less money is spent on actual construction than is paid out to construction contractors. And consequently it behooves the financially minded to own construction companies; the larger the project, the greater the rip-off.

The celebrated "construction scheme" was successfully carried out in mid–nineteenth century France by an outfit called the Société Générale de Crédit Mobilier. This holding company siphoned off its profits from the construction of public works.

Durant and others saw that a similar scheme could be carried out in the construction of American railroads. They set up the Credit Mobilier of America to build the Union Pacific. An identical outfit was set up to rake off funds from the Central Pacific.

And a similar scheme was used over a century later to bilk the Penn Central.

While the Union Pacific itself would be a big, widely held corporation with many hundreds of stockholders, the construction firm would be a small, closely held company where the few owners could reap vast profits by overcharging the railroad.

The Credit Mobilier built 667 miles of Union Pacific track, charging about $50,000 per mile for construction actually costing closer to $30,000. This process nearly bankrupted the Union Pacific. It netted the Credit Mobilier somewhere between $7 million and $23 million, a staggering amount in those days.

Dee Brown quotes a contemporary description by Charles Francis Adams: "Who then constitutes the Credit Mobilier? It is but another name for the Pacific Railroad ring. The members of it are in Congress; they are trustees for the bondholders, they are directors, they are stockholders, they are contractors; in Washington they vote the subsidies, in New York they receive them, upon the Plains they expend them, and in the Credit Mobilier they divide them. . . . Under one name or another a ring of some seventy persons is struck at whatever point the Union Pacific is approached. As stockholders they own the road, as mortgagees they have a lien upon it, as directors they contract for its construction, and as members of the Credit Mobilier they build it."

In this and similar ways the greatest ruling-class fortunes of nineteenth-century America were built on the railroads.

The vast wealth and power that could be made led to an equally vast *overbuilding of railroads:* "Whenever on a map two towns could be found with no railroad running between them," Brown writes, "some clever sharper would appear to organize a railroad company. . . . It did not matter whether the towns had anything to ship to each other. . . .

"Railroad construction became a mania in the 1880s with feeder lines, branch lines, and short lines running in all directions. . . .

"So much of the public's money was poured into unplanned and often unneeded railroads in the West that the inhabitants of the region were burdened with sharply rising taxes extending far into the future. For shouldering this debt they received poor service and high freight rates, which were another form of taxation. Westerners slowly began to perceive that the real purpose of the railroad builders was not to provide transportation for passengers and freight but to issue and manipulate railroad stocks and bonds."

The Pennsylvania and 1877

The Pennsylvania Railroad rose to even greater financial heights in the nineteenth century than Vanderbilt's New York Central. For a time it was not only the largest private enterprise in the United States but also the biggest freight carrier in the world.

In 1873 it employed 200,000 workers. By the turn of the century the Pennsylvania also controlled the Chesapeake and Ohio, Baltimore and Ohio, Reading, and Norfolk and Western railroads, as well as vast coal fields.

This trust was controlled from the start by the Philadelphia aristocracy. Founded in 1846, the Pennsylvania's original board of directors consisted of six merchants, four manufacturers, and two bankers—all Philadelphians.

The inestimable wealth that these and subsequent financiers raked off the Pennsylvania can still be glimpsed if one visits the "Main Line" mansions in Philadelphia's western suburbs. There generations of Pennsylvania Railroad owners have lived in great stone structures surrounded by mighty trees, formal gardens, and rolling lawns.

The Pennsylvania Railroad Company paid dividends every year without fail from 1856 to 1969. It paid 10 percent dividends in 1864 and 1865, despite the Civil War. It paid 10 percent dividends in 1874 and 8 percent in 1875 and 1876, as the country wallowed in its first major depression. The "Pennsy" paid 8 percent in 1930 and 6.5 percent in 1931, as the United States sank into the Great Depression of the 1930s.

And the same company is still a major factor in the hidden control of Amtrak and Conrail, as we will see in a later chapter.

The power of the Pennsylvania was personified in the last quarter of the nineteenth century in the character of its president, Thomas Scott. Scott "owned" the Pennsylvania legislature in Harrisburg and was not too far from exercising the same control in Washington.

Union Station in downtown Washington near the Capitol was originally a terminal of the Pennsylvania Railroad, and it is a monument to the power this company once held in Congress.

It was Scott who engineered the 1877 compromise making Rutherford Hayes the U.S. president. In the 1876 elections, Republican Hayes lost to Democrat Samuel Tilden. But the results were contested in some southern states. Ultimately, some southern Democrats shifted over to supporting Hayes and turned the election results around.

Scott promised these Democrats that the new government would back the "Texas and Pacific Railroad," a project to build a transcontinental route through the Southwest. This would give southern capital its own route to the West in competition with such northern lines as the Union Pacific and the Northern Pacific.

We saw in the previous chapter that Scott purchased the labor of Black prisoners at a few cents a day to race the construction of the Texas and Pacific line across Texas.

"It is hardly an accident that on March 2, 1877, when Hayes received the telegram confirming his election, he was en route to Washington in Tom Scott's own luxurious private car," writes labor historian Philip Foner.

In their rush west, the railroads inevitably overbuilt. Stocks and bonds were sold in companies building railroads through barely inhabited land—and often in companies merely promising to build such roads. On top of this, the railroads that were under construction poured millions into the coffers of corrupt construction companies such as the Credit Mobilier, subjecting the overextended companies to all the greater financial duress.

In 1873 the worst financial and economic crash that the country had yet seen was touched off by the failure of Jay Cooke and Company, a banking firm attempting to build the Northern Pacific Railroad across the far North. Cooke's failure ignited a panic.

The New York Stock Exchange closed for ten days beginning September 20. By the end of the year, eighty-nine railroads had defaulted on their bonds. Railroad construction collapsed, throwing a half-million workers into unemployment. Breadlines spread in the major cities, and farm prices also collapsed, although the railroads continued to press high rates on the desperate farmers.

Year after year during the depression, the railroads continued to lay off workers and to slash the wages of those who remained. By 1877 rail wages had already been cut 30 to 40 percent. A new round of wage reductions began in June, when the Pennsylvania cut another 10 percent.

But when the Baltimore and Ohio put through its 10 percent wage cut July 16, it touched off a strike by B&O workers in Martinsburg, West Virginia. That strike of a handful of firemen grew into one of the great labor upsurges of history—a national strike by railroad workers that spread from city to city and line to line, and a strike that in some big American cities deepened into a general strike, supported by all the working populace.

Philip Foner gives a detailed account of this strike in *The Great Labor Uprising of 1877*. Battles were fought in city after city. Each of them contains useful lessons for present and future labor struggles—some of which will be against exactly the same railroad trusts.

This was the first strike in which the federal government used major military force to support the companies against their employees. Tom Scott recommended a "rifle diet" for the strikers, and it was used—not only against the strikers but also against masses of their civilian supporters.

Big battles occurred in Baltimore, Philadelphia, St. Louis, Cincinnati, and Chicago. The biggest, in Pittsburgh, captures the spirit of that memorable struggle against monopoly rule.

"By 1877," Foner writes, "hatred of the Pennsylvania Railroad had permeated all classes in Pittsburgh. . . ." The company refused to equip its freight trains with safety devices, and during the depression it made work on the main line more hazardous by doubling the size of its trains and reducing the number of men who worked on them."

Railroad strikers took over the Pittsburgh yards July 19, and no trains left the city for more than a week. A militia was raised in Philadelphia to crush the strike.

"Saturday, July 21, a day long to be remembered by Pittsburghers, dawned bright and beautiful," Foner writes. "The strikers had remained stationed along the line during the entire night. Early the next morning, they were joined

In 1877, the people of Pittsburgh put the property of the Pennsylvania Railroad to the torch.

by rolling-mill men, mechanics, the unemployed, and women and children."

This assemblage defending the strike was assaulted that afternoon by the Philadelphia troops. When the command to fire rang out, "immediately the troops began firing directly into the crowd. The panic-stricken men, women, and children, trapped and unarmed, surged in all directions, and several fell. . . .

"Within a few minutes, at least twenty were dead. . . ."

That evening the people of Pittsburgh put the property of the Pennsylvania Railroad to the torch.

In the next days the troops again fired into civilian demonstrations that now raged throughout the city.

In the Chicago strike, says Foner, "The tensions between Irish and Czech workers, as sharp as any in the city, suddenly became irrelevant in the common battle against the police, the authorities, and the 'respectable citizens.'"

Everywhere, however, the striking populace met the bullets of troops and police. The two-week-long insurrection against the railroad owners was crushed in blood. Hundreds of strike leaders were arrested and imprisoned.

President Hayes wrote in his diary, August 5, "The strikers have been put down by *force*. . . ."

In these battles socialists, newly organized into the Workingmen's Party of the United States, played leading roles wherever they could. In Cincinnati, Peter Clark, a Black socialist, was a chief organizer of the resistance. There and in St. Louis, large numbers of Black workers fought in the strikes.

Albert Parsons, then a young radical in Chicago, addressed huge audiences as an avowed revolutionary and enemy of railroad magnates Scott and Vanderbilt. Parsons would later become a martyr for his role in the eight-hour day movement after the Haymarket protests of working people in Chicago in May 1886.

But in 1877 the railroad workers and their allies were virtually unorganized. They could not wage an effective resistance against the brutal onslaught of the employers and their government. Strike leaders were fired and blacklisted. Fledgling unions sprang up in the struggle only to disappear afterwards, for the most part. The railroads were soon to enter into one of the most spectacular and profitable booms in American history.

Debs and the 1894 Pullman Strike

The railroad companies helped turn a young fireman into one of the greatest American labor leaders and revolutionary socialists: Eugene V. Debs.

Debs was an early builder of the craft-divided railroad unions, a pioneer in the struggle for industry-wide unionism, and the most popular leader of the American socialist movement until his death in 1926. He ran as a socialist candidate for president five times, polling nearly one million votes from his jail cell in the 1920 presidential elections.

Debs's history, as told by his biographer Ray Ginger and his speeches collected in *Eugene V. Debs Speaks*, is an important manual for the struggles of railroad workers today. As the companies deepen their attack on railroad jobs and working conditions, more and more workers will want to study these rich lessons of the past.

They will find that the real Debsian tradition is nothing like the image projected by many union officials today. Debs found bureaucracy odious, he turned down the salary raises voted by the ranks countless times, and he was a class-struggle fighter from beginning to end.

Once Debs became a convinced socialist, he completely rejected the idea of voting for "friends of labor" Democrats or Republicans. On the contrary, he believed that independent labor political action against the ruling capitalist parties was the most important step labor could take.

Debs, who came out of Terre Haute, Indiana, worked as a fireman for the Vandalia line from age fifteen to nineteen. The hazardous working conditions of the railroads made a lasting impression on him.

"Several railroads," according to Ginger, "used unsafe equipment in order to cut their operating costs. . . . Faulty trestles collapsed under passing trains. A poor coupling system caused many railroaders to be smashed between cars. . . .

"Finally, in the autumn of 1874, one of Eugene's friends slipped under a locomotive and was killed." From that year on Debs worked tirelessly, first to build the Brotherhood of Locomotive Firemen, after that to try to build a federation of railroad unions, and finally, to build the socialist movement.

After some ten years of working for the BLF, Debs recognized that little headway could be made in the struggle against the railroad trusts by isolated craft unions—especially when most had no-strike clauses.

Beginning in the late 1880s Debs traveled up and down the rails and across the country campaigning for federation of the railroad unions and for the right to strike.

At a national convention of brakemen in 1888, Debs declared that when "we come in contact with a narrow minded, bigoted and infamous railroad official, who will not accord us our common rights, then I am in favor of strikes. Why, my friends, there is not a star or a stripe in our national flag that does not tell of a strike, not one. From Lexington, from Concord . . . clear down to Yorktown, is one succession of strikes for liberty and independence. . . ."

At that time, the fledgling trade union movement faced all-out repression. For example, in the spring of 1892, steel magnate Henry Frick ordered Pinkerton agents to open fire on the strikers at Carnegie Steel's Homestead works in Pennsylvania, killing seven men. Eight thousand state troopers then seized the plant. Homestead strike leaders were indicted for murder, aggravated riot, conspiracy, and treason. In a single stroke the steel trust had broken the power of one of the strongest craft unions of the time. Similar violence was soon used to crush silver miners at Coeur d'Alene, Idaho, and to establish a nonunion shop there.

In 1892 Debs resigned from the BLF. As he later explained the impasse of craft unionism, "You can never succeed with the men divided in separate organizations. If engineers have a grievance the firemen will have one. An injury to one should be an injury to all. It is wrong to be separate. The corporations do not take this view of it; when a road becomes involved in a strike the other roads, the newspapers, the banks and all the rest come to the rescue. I wish that labor might follow the example set by capital."

Beginning in 1892-93 the country slipped into a new depression, even worse than that of 1873-77. Once again, overbuilding of the railroads and subsequent railroad bankruptcies were the main economic factor causing the depression.

"Factories closed," writes Ginger. "Families were evicted from their homes. Mothers plundered garbage cans in their search for food. Children were turned out to forage for themselves. Highways and city streets were clogged with wandering, homeless, barefoot men."

Debs and the other most farsighted railroad union leaders responded with the formation of the American Railway Union, open to workers from all the crafts. But in a dangerous concession to the racism of the period, Blacks were excluded.

Debs later said of this disastrous policy, "The leaders of the opposition [to Black membership] proved subsequently to have been traitors to the union, sent to the convention, doubtless, at the instigation of the corporations to defeat the unity of the working class."

The top officials of the railroad unions were united in their opposition to the ARU. Samuel Gompers, head of the American Federation of Labor, opposed it too. All of them feared losing craft union privileges to a militant and aroused rank and file. Despite this the ARU grew by leaps and bounds.

"It seemed," Ginger writes, "that every underpaid railroader in the country—and there were nearly a million of them—wanted to join the order. . . . Entire lodges of the Railway Carmen and the Switchmen transferred to the ARU. Firemen, conductors, even engineers, joined the industrial union. But the great majority of recruits came from previously unorganized men who had been unable to meet the high monthly dues of the Brotherhoods. The unskilled workers had been unprotected, underpaid, exploited; now the dikes snapped and a reservoir of bitterness and hope drove men pell-mell into the American Railway Union."

The first test of the ARU was a strike against James J. Hill's Great Northern. The union emerged victorious in that battle, which was the only important industrial strike

National Guard in action in the 1894 Pullman strike (above).
Eugene V. Debs (below) giving antiwar speech June 16, 1918, in
Canton, Ohio. For this he was sentenced to ten years in prison.

won in that period. A short time later the ARU became deadlocked in one of the bitterest battles ever against the owners of an American corporation: the Pullman boycott of 1894.

Like all workers in those days, the workers at George Pullman's sleeping-car company were faced with sharp wage cutbacks and layoffs. But on top of this, Pullman, Illinois, was a company town. The jobless and poverty-stricken workers had to continue paying rent to the company for their houses and going into deeper debt to the company as the depression intensified.

In May 1894 the workers went on strike. And they called on the ARU for help. The militant workers of the new industrial union demanded and carried out a national boycott of trains carrying Pullman cars.

The American ruling class responded with fury. In Chicago, where the ARU was headquartered, newspapers lied about and blasted Debs day in and day out. "Strike is Now War," the Chicago *Tribune* declared. A caption over its editorial said:

"Six Days Shalt Thou Labor —Bible

"Not Unless I Say So —Debs"

Court injunctions were used for the first time in a major way to punish supporters of the Pullman strike. The railroad companies bought lawyers and judges by the bushel.

Railroad spies followed Debs wherever he went. ARU members—including Debs—were fired, blacklisted, and imprisoned. (The lawyer most responsible for landing Debs in the Cook County Jail in Chicago worked for the Chicago, Milwaukee and St. Paul Railroad, predecessor of the present-day job-slashing Milwaukee Road.)

And Grover Cleveland, the Democratic president for whom Debs had earlier campaigned, sent the army into Chicago to crush the strike.

The armed strike-breakers incited violence. Innocent people were murdered—and the ARU was blamed. The U.S. government and state troops, the police and courts, and the opposition of the railroad brotherhoods themselves ultimately crushed the Pullman boycott and along with it the ARU itself.

But by this time the ARU and the Pullman fight had gained the attention and support of working people everywhere. The concept of the potential power of industrial unionism was afoot in the land.

After the battle, Gene Debs spent a six-month term in jail studying, among other things, socialism. This study and subsequent thought helped Debs see through the railroad companies to the capitalist system itself—its government, its parties, and its courts, all of which front for the railroad trusts. Looking back on the ARU experience, Debs said, "I had yet to learn the workings of the capitalist system, the resources of its masters and the weakness of its slaves."

When President Cleveland and the railroads conspired to crush the Pullman boycott in 1894 Debs said, "there was delivered, from wholly unexpected quarters, a swift succession of blows that blinded me for an instant and then opened wide my eyes—and in the gleam of every bayonet and the flash of every rifle *the class struggle was revealed.* That was my first practical lesson in socialism, though wholly unaware that it was called by that name."

Debs subsequently campaigned for almost three decades, until his death, to build a mass revolutionary party of workers to overthrow American capitalism.

Craft Unionism

The first two decades of this century saw intensified attacks on workers, the deepening open-shop drive of the ruling industrialists, and a mass wave of working-class radicalization in response to this ruling-class attack. The socialist movement grew rapidly. During the 1902 strike by anthracite coal miners in eastern Pennsylvania, according to labor historian Philip Foner, "In the strike region, the Pennsylvania Socialists were gaining recruits at a phenomenal rate. Four Socialist locals were established every day after mid-July, and within a few weeks, the membership of these locals increased from 25 to 340 each."

In the same period the craft union officialdom hardened as an opponent of radical social change. It fought industrial unionism and became an increasingly important pillar of capitalist rule within the working class. The craft unions played an important role in a process that will be analyzed in the next few chapters.

There were two million railroad workers in America as the twentieth century opened. They included tens of thousands who had participated in the 1894 Pullman struggle. Despite the severe repression that followed that defeat, Eugene Debs was revered as a railroad labor leader. The militant ranks of railroad workers soon forced lasting concessions from the mighty owners of the industry. Railroad unionization spread. Workers won higher wages and standardized contracts, concerning both wages and working conditions. They were also able to gain some safety protection.

Yet this process seemed to halt midway. By the 1920s railroad workers had won most of the major work rules that they have today—gains that are now being undermined. In 1926 railroad workers were saddled with federal strike-breaking provisions which they have not been able to push aside. Railroad workers remain divided along craft lines, weakening their power in the face of unified owners. The craft union bureaucracy bears a heavy responsibility for this straitjacketing of railroad labor.

The craft brotherhoods had originated as insurance organizations. The jobs were so dangerous that other insurance was inaccessible to railroad workers. The Locomotive Engineers brotherhood was formed in 1863, and Locomotive Firemen in 1873. These were among the earliest unions formed.

Statistics underline the dangers of working on the railroads. In 1900, 2,550 railroad workers were killed and 39,643 injured. The figures for 1910 were 3,382 dead, 95,671 injured. Insurance was consequently needed to help support the families of the dead and injured, but the dominant insurance-agency character of the unions helped pave the way for business unionism and bureaucratism. The dues could support increasingly higher salaries, and ultimately capitalist investment from the union funds. The agents and officials became increasingly aloof from a rank and file constantly on the road.

Their primary responsibility, these officials believed, was to assure the capitalists of organized labor's cooperation (or rather subservience), both within industry and at the governmental level. In return, they assumed, grateful employers would make a few concessions to the workers. Sensitivity to ruling-class needs made the bureaucrats loath to lead significant struggles against the ruling class in defense of workers' interests.*

They concentrated on strengthening their own power at the top of the narrow crafts they presided over.

"There was scarcely a convention of the A. F. of L., even in the 1890's, where some discussion of the need for . . . change was not part of the proceedings," according to Foner. Opponents of craft unionism explained its inability to adjust to rapidly changing industrial conditions, which were bringing more and more workers under the sway of a single corporation. They also pointed out how much of an

---

*See "Mentality of a Union Bureaucrat" in *Teamster Politics* by Farrell Dobbs. Dobbs's four-volume series on the Teamsters includes an invaluable guide to the role of bureaucracy in the trade union movement.

advantage it was to the owners of these corporations to be able to negotiate separately with the different crafts and to play one against the other. Jurisdictional disputes between the craft unions also played into the bosses' hands. As more and more unskilled and semiskilled workers poured into the labor force, however, the AFL and the railroad brotherhoods stiffened their defense of the entrenched privileges of the most highly skilled minority. Railroad engineers were the highest-paid workers of the time. They considered themselves an aristocracy within the aristocracy of skilled workers. Within the railroad system they could look down on a whole hierarchy of laborers stretching from the track maintenance crews to the blacksmiths, boilermakers, and carmen in the shops. The operating brotherhoods refused to join the AFL.

Whereas the AFL unions effectively kept Black workers out through insurmountably high dues and other implicitly discriminatory methods, the constitutions of the railroad brotherhoods explicitly excluded Blacks. Craft union discrimination was an important factor in the reaction of the 1890s which followed the post–Civil War Reconstruction. Black labor had played an important role in southern railroading, shipping, and building. Beginning in the late 1890s, Blacks were steadily eliminated from skilled jobs. Women and immigrant workers were also kept out of the craft unions. For decades the operating brotherhoods and AFL craft unions were lily white.

The American ruling class also fostered the conservatizing of the top layer of craft union leadership. In 1900 Ohio industrialist Mark Hanna formed the National Civic Federation (NCF) to bring managers and union leaders together. An NCF official stated in 1903: "Our experience has convinced us that the best way to control labor organizations is to lead and not to force them. We are also convinced that the conservative element in all unions will control when properly led and officered."

Samuel Gompers, president of the AFL, John Mitchell, president of the United Mine Workers, and the heads of the railroad brotherhoods were charter NCF members. "The interests of labor and capital are one and the same," these labor misleaders preached as money poured into NCF coffers from J. P. Morgan & Co., Andrew Carnegie, U.S. Steel Corp., and other sectors of capitalist monopoly.

The "labor lieutenants of capital" were played up in the bourgeois press. A *Saturday Evening Post* article in 1910, for example, hailed P. H. Morrissey, who had headed the Brotherhood of Railroad Trainmen for fourteen years. Morrissey had told the *Post*, "We want to teach railroad employees, first of all, that they are as vitally interested in stopping the flood of hostile legislation as are the railroad corporations themselves. . . . You can't hurt the railroads without hurting them." This put Morrissey on the side of the railroad owners not only against workers, but also against the farmers, ranchers, and small businessmen who were pressing Congress for legislation to control the gouging railroads.

Meanwhile, if contract negotiations broke down between railroad employees and the employer, the bureaucrats would try to settle the matter through arbitration. If arbitration failed, and they were pushed toward a strike, they still delayed. Every effort was made to "cool off hotheads" and give full play to any expression of hesitation that might emanate from the ranks. This bureaucratic mood was vividly expressed by Warren Stone, the Grand Chief of the Brotherhood of Locomotive Engineers, in Chicago hearings on railroad wages in 1915. Stone pleaded with the arbitration board:

"I also want to say, neither in the way of explanation nor excuse, that the grand officers of this organization, instead of taking the lid off, try to keep the brake on, and we are not imagining these grievances. If the men did not come to us with these grievances we would not be here with them. And the thing we have always tried to do is to be conservative and keep the dissension down. . . . We do not dream these things and if we simply take the brake off and let the men go, it would be a whole lot more radical that what it is."

At the arbitration hearing where Stone was speaking there was one other representative of the railroad unions, two spokesmen for the companies, and two supposedly neutral members. The poet Carl Sandburg reported on this meeting in the *International Socialist Review*. Sandburg satirized the concept of neutral arbitrators. "Most important of all, naturally," said Sandburg, "are the names and personalities of the two 'umpires'. . . . On the tongues inside these two heads rests the inevitable and irrevocable

LITTLE BROTHERS OF THE RICH.

Cartoon from the *International Socialist Review* shows United Mine Workers chief John Mitchell, AFL head Samuel Gompers, and New York financier August Belmont, head of the National Civil Federation.

say-so as to how much more money the payrolls shall hold
for 65,000 engine workers. . . .

"One is Charles Nagel. He is a lawyer from St. Louis.
His special distinction that fitted him for the place of
umpire was gained as a member of the cabinet of President
Taft. . . . It was as Secretary Nagel that he formed close
association with steamship interests and the importation
of a labor supply from Europe. . . .

"Jeter C. Pritchard is the other 'umpire.' He is a judge of
the United States District Court which sits in Richmond,
Virginia. . . .

"So there we are—two Republican lawyers, office-
holders, appointed to fat jobs under Republican Presidents
Taft and Roosevelt, are going to say the last word on
wages and labor conditions on ninety-eight western rail-
ways."

And so the cards were stacked entirely against the rank-
and-file workers.

Eugene Debs wrote in the *International Socialist Review*
in February 1911: "The point I wish to make and drive
home with all the force I can is that it is the rank and file,
the common workers, who are always the victims of craft
unionism. . . .

"And while these poor devils are facing the automatic
revolvers of the detectives and having their heads beaten
into pulp by the police, and while their families are being
evicted for non-payment of rent and their children are
suffering for bread, their grand leaders are banqueting
with the plutocratic lords and dames under the prostituted
auspices of the Civic Federation of Labor, making merry
over the beatitudes that flow from the brotherhood of
capital and labor, and glorifying the marvelous triumphs
of trade unionism in the United States."

*   *   *

Pressures toward amalgamation of the railroad crafts
have flared up again and again. A noteworthy struggle to
amalgamate the Brotherhood of Locomotive Engineers
and the Brotherhood of Locomotive Firemen and Enginemen grew out of the post–Second World War labor upsurge
in 1946, although it was defeated in 1949. A detailed
account is given by George Novack, in his unpublished

1958 monograph "Unity Caucus on the Railroads: The Story of the Consolidation Committee of Enginemen." In 1969 the Brotherhood of Railroad Trainmen, the Brotherhood of Locomotive Firemen and Enginemen, the Order of Railway Conductors and Brakemen, and the Switchmen's Union of North America did merge to form the United Transportation Union, the largest of the railroad unions today.

Rebellion and Reaction: 1919-1924

The First World War set a syndrome of capital-labor-government encounters that served to dampen working-class militancy and to push back the labor movement that had been rising before the war. It was followed by fresh outbursts of labor struggles comparable to the 1946 strike wave following World War II. And in another parallel, both postwar labor upsurges spurred violent reaction by the ruling class. In 1919 Washington launched an anti-labor drive accompanied by witch-hunt and anticommunist hysteria it would not match again until the McCarthyite witch-hunt of the cold war.

In 1919 over four million workers struck. During a general strike in Seattle, workers prevented U.S. arms from being shipped to Russia where they were to be used in the imperialists' attempt to crush the new workers' state led by Lenin and the Bolsheviks. There was a 300,000-strong steelworker strike beginning in September, and in November the coal miners went out. The threat of a federal injunction kept railworkers from striking nationally but there were local walkouts.

In the same year the railroad labor movement launched a drive to nationalize the railroads, which was applauded by the 1919 United Mine Workers convention and endorsed by the AFL, over Gompers's objections.

The nationalization plan was drafted by a Chicago lawyer named Glen Plumb. Washington had taken over the railroads during the war in 1917 and had been forced to grant railroad workers significant concessions, including wage increases. According to Edward Keating, a Democratic congressman from Colorado and a journalist, the main proposals of the "Plumb Plan" were:

1. That the federal government should renationalize all

the lines so as to give the entire nation a unified and efficient system.

2. Stockholders would be given cash or 4 percent government bonds for the value of their holdings.

3. The roads would be operated by a tripartite commission of fifteen members—five representing the public, five the operating officials, and five the employees.

4. Fifty percent of the profits would go to the officials and employees of the railroads in the form of higher pay; the other fifty percent would go to the public in reduced freight and passenger rates.

5. The operating officials were to become "free men, no longer subject to banker control."

6. The workers, without regard to craft, were to be permitted to organize into unions of their choice.

Keating wrote that the plan was drafted "with the approval of all the Standard Railroad Labor Organizations, with the exception of the Brotherhood of Railroad Trainmen. . . .

"The labor leaders who supported it were not Socialists, neither was Mr. Plumb. Perhaps one or two of the labor chieftains had been associated with the Socialist Party in their youth, but the others were Jeffersonian Democrats, or Lincoln Republicans, or plain Independents, and the economic and political views of the big majority were extremely moderate."

Keating himself launched in 1919 the rail union newspaper *Labor* as the newspaper of the "Plumb Plan League."

The plan had many weaknesses. To keep the railroads on a profit-making basis would inevitably pit them against the workers, passengers, and farmers they should serve. To compensate the former owners would be to load down the nationalized rail system with a formidable debt that would stand in the way of expansion and improvement. The Plumb Plan also accepted the fraudulent notion of a neutral governing board—ignoring what railroad labor history had already proved: that the so-called public members of these boards actually represented capitalist interests. They were invariably executives of other corporations, professors, or lawyers, whose allegiances just as invariably were procapitalist and antilabor.

All of these weaknesses flowed from the classcollaborationist viewpoint of its authors. For the railroad union officials, everything was tied to winning the votes of capitalist politicians in Washington. The unions campaigned for these politicians, going all out to line up the railroad labor vote for them. They lobbied with them. They had no perspective of mobilizing the ranks of labor *independently* of the Democrats and Republicans in order to build a mass base to force the demands of workers through Washington. (In fact, in 1921-25 these same railroad officials played an important role in blocking the formation of a labor party that was pushed at that time by leaders of the Socialist Party and sections of the AFL.)

In any event the Plumb Plan was washed away in the flood tide of reaction that soon swept over the United States. The winter of 1919-20 saw a wave of repression against the socialist and trade union movements, including arrests, imprisonments, and deportations launched by Democratic Attorney General A. Mitchell Palmer. "Before the first World War," according to historian Theodore Draper, "only two states, New York and Tennessee, had laws against 'sedition,' and no one had ever been prosecuted under them. After the war, thirty-five states passed legislation against 'sedition,' 'criminal anarchy,' 'criminal syndicalism,' and the like. An epidemic of prosecutions broke out. . . .

"Thousands were rounded up in raids on homes and meetings. The hysteria communicated itself to school boards, college presidents, self-constituted 'vigilante committees,' and pulpits. Spies and secret agents infested the labor movement in behalf of the big corporations."

In January 1920 Palmer initiated raids in thirty-three cities. Over five thousand arrests were made. There were hundreds of convictions and some deportations.

Meanwhile the 1919 steel strike had been crushed with such violence that it took several decades for steel workers to recoup their forces. The antiunion drive was being pressed everywhere. Armies of thugs roamed the coal fields and other industries, beating up and killing workers who were fighting for unions. Wages were drastically slashed and farm prices dropped menacingly.

The Railroad Labor Board decreed an 11 percent cut in wages in June 1921 and another cut by as much as 20 percent in the wages for nonoperating crafts in early 1922.

An explosion of resistance broke out in the mines and on the railroads in the spring and summer of 1922. In April more than 500,000 coal miners walked off their jobs. On July 1 400,000 railroad shopworkers struck. It was the first nationwide rail strike since 1894. By July 15, 600,000 roundhouse workers were out—boilermakers, blacksmiths, machinists, carmen, electrical workers, sheetmetal workers, stationary firemen. *Labor* newspaper reported an additional 100,000 volunteers in the strike from other crafts and including unorganized workers.

From San Bernadino, California, a woman's auxiliary reported in the July 15 issue of *Labor,* "We are doing effective work on the picket line, also visiting the homes of the few that did not respond. Our children's future is at stake, and we are going to win."

The July 20 issue of *Labor* recounted how farmers in five counties of Texas had adopted resolutions supporting the miners' strike and filled trucks up with food to help feed the miners' children.

The September 16 *Labor* noted a study on food costs prepared at the University of Minnesota: Even with the most rigorous economy, bread and butter and meat alone would cost a family of five $505.96 a year and "if only the bare necessities of a decent minimum standard of living were supplied the cost would be from $1,692.50 to $1,733.38." Railroad shopworkers were receiving $563 a year.

Yet the shop-craft strike was smashed. The operating crafts refused to join. If they took such a militant step, they argued, they would lose the support of the politicians in Washington they catered to. "If we behave, we can persuade President Harding to settle the strike on favorable terms," was the gist of their policy. Harding responded by sending the new attorney general, Harry Daugherty, to Chicago, where Daugherty obtained one of the most sweeping antilabor injunctions in American history. Federal Judge James Wilkerson issued a restraining order against the strikes that prohibited union officials from "picketing or in any manner by letters, circulars, telephone messages, word of mouth, or interviews encouraging any person to leave the employ of a railroad!"

Although some strikes lasted throughout 1923 and into 1924 the majority were settled by the "Chicago agreement" of September 1922. This neither restored wages to earlier levels nor won the union shop the shop-craft workers had demanded. A large number of railroad companies refused to hire back the strikers and many fostered the formation of company unions.

The steel defeat in 1919 and the defeat of the railroad shop crafts in 1922 were two stunning blows that helped pave the way for more than a decade of "labor peace"—the peace of the graveyard. Workers and farmers alike were swept toward the oncoming depression. No important new gains would be won until the great battles for industrial unionism in the 1930s. The railroad labor movement would never regain the momentum it lost in the 1920s.

Railway Labor Act

Railroad workers are saddled with the most complex labor laws on the books. The Railway Labor Act imposes a barrier to strikes for which there is little parallel elsewhere in U.S. industry. The processes that brought this about had mostly been completed by the mid-1920s.

To understand them it might be helpful to step back and ask what, indeed, are the interests of capital and wage labor on the railroads? Are they identical—or conflicting? We have already seen the drastic wage cuts that took place in the early 1920s. Real wages of railroad workers—the actual purchasing power of their wages after taking inflation into account—were lower in 1926 than in 1915.

From the standpoint of shipping freight, the maximum return comes to the carriers if the freight cars are shipped only when they are full and as soon as they are loaded. The longer the trains and the lower the number of workers, the more profitable. The most efficient crew is one that is there at the moment the trains are loaded, ready to transport them. Labor is not needed when the freight cars are empty and it is not needed when there are no cars around.

Leaving aside the question of railroad safety, which is the subject of a later chapter, the history of the railway labor movement to a large degree is the history of the struggle of railroad workers against the profit needs of shippers. Railroad workers had to struggle for some limit on the number of hours they worked, and then to struggle for a sixteen-hour day, and then an eight-hour day. They had to struggle for workdays that begin at fixed times. They had to struggle for overtime pay. And many railroad workers are still subjected to "extra boards" or other arbitrary working schedules where they do not know when they may be called in or for how long.

As recently as 1979 in California the Southern Pacific tried to restore arbitrary layover times for workers. It was not enough they should work these difficult schedules five or six days, but they wouldn't be able to determine which days they get off. "It's inhuman. It breaks up families," young Southern Pacific workers declared.

The size of the crews is a ceaseless struggle on the railroads.

Workers in the operating crafts had to fight for mileage limits so they would not have to go so far away from home that they could not return regularly. These limits were extended with the advance of railroad technology and the long straightaways in the West, but they remain vital to a stable livelihood for road workers.

The struggle over wages and working conditions increasingly brought railroad workers head on against the U.S. government. From the 1880s, every single national rail labor struggle, many regional struggles, and even struggles against a particular railroad company have brought on the direct intervention of the federal government. Congress has enacted railway labor laws since the 1880s; comparable legislation in other industries did not occur until the 1930s. And there is still no other industry where workers are so engulfed in federal laws.

These are enforced because of the economic, military, and political centrality of railroads to the U.S. economy. Even today, when there is considerable trucking and some air freight, railroads are vital to U.S. industry and agriculture. Not only farming and agribusiness but also coal, oil, nuclear energy, chemicals, and auto depend on rail. The railroads were obviously all the more central at the turn of the century before automobile use became widespread and when there were no interstate highways.

Ever since the Civil War, the U.S. military has paid close attention to this means of transportation. Federal troops intervened directly to crush the 1877 rebellion. The railroads were nationalized during World War I, and Presidents Roosevelt, Truman, and Eisenhower all threatened army seizure of the railroads whenever major negotiations broke down.

We have already seen the political power of the railroad trusts in Washington. Eugene Debs became a socialist after President Grover Cleveland ordered the troops against him in Chicago in 1894. Debs saw that what tied the police, the courts, the newspapers, and the federal government together were the *class interests* of the owners of railroads, which all these institutions defended. Every measure of protection railroad workers gained—whether it involved improving the hand brakes that threw railroad workers to their deaths, or standardizing the hours of work—was gained in struggle against the railroad companies and increasingly against the government. Each new struggle of railroad workers was greeted in Washington by renewed efforts to *legally deprive railroad workers of the right to strike.*

• The Arbitration Act of 1888 set up the initial government machinery for the investigation of railroad labor disputes and established commissions of arbitration. The conclusions of these commissions, however, did not have binding power.

• The Erdman Act of 1898 replaced the Arbitration Act, introducing federal courts into the arbitration process. This also had provisions for the Interstate Commerce Commission to appoint a "neutral" member of the arbitration committee.

• The Newlands Act of July 1913 established the United States Board of Mediation and Conciliation, appointed by the president, as a permanent mediation group.

• The United States Railroad Administration was established by President Woodrow Wilson in December 1917 when he took over the railroads. Even before this, a significant concession had been granted railroad workers in the Adamson Act, which established the eight-hour day. The government railroad boards made other concessions in standardizing wages and working rules and in hiring Blacks, immigrants, and women in the shop crafts. At the same time this process legitimized the shop-craft union divisions as the various craft unions negotiated with the government.

• The 1920 Transportation Act established a presidentially appointed tripartite U.S. Railroad Board with near-to-dictatorial powers over wages, work rules, and working conditions. It was this board's decisions in 1920-21 to revise the wartime laws, abolishing overtime pay for work on Sundays and holidays, amalgamating shop-craft jobs, eliminating point-away-from-home pay, making drastic wage slashes, and reversing other gains, that precipitated the 1922 strike.

Such an overview helps to bring out the obstructive character of these government agencies and laws. The "United States Board of Mediation and Conciliation" of 1913 sounds like a marble-columned edifice imbued from time immemorial with legal authority. And so the authorities would like workers to believe. In fact it was a passing phenomenon in the struggle between railroad workers and the owners, reached in a compromise between the owners' government and the railroad union leaderships, at a particular moment of the class struggle. The Railway Labor Act of 1926 is no less a product of the relationship of forces between the corporations and the workers. Even though it has been on the books for over half a century and is still frequently invoked by presidents against railroad workers, this congressional act grew out of the changing class struggle. New motion on the part of the railroad union ranks can shove it aside.

From the 1880s on, Washington pressed its effort to deprive railroad workers of their legal right to strike. But even the harsh Transportation Act of 1920, passed in the heat of anticommunist hysteria, did not give the government the legal right to halt strikes. It was Attorney General Daugherty's 1922 injunction against the striking shop-craft workers that went the furthest toward legally embodying the notion that railroad workers do not have an unqualified right to strike. This notion became law in the Railway Labor Act.

Defeat of the shop-craft strikers put wind in the sails of the railroad companies and their representatives in Washington. They pressed for new legislation. Following several years of behind-the-scenes negotiations with the railroad brotherhood officials, Congress produced the Railway Labor Act, signed into law by President Calvin Coolidge on May 20, 1926.

This law provided the main outlines for the machinery to arbitrate railroad labor disputes that is still in effect today. A new Board of Mediation was instituted, consisting of five members appointed by the president.

If this board fails to produce a settlement it is required to try to influence the parties to submit to arbitration. If they agree, an arbitration board is established. If they fail to agree, the mediation board notifies the president to create an emergency board to make a report within thirty days; and after the report another thirty days ensue in which strikes or lockouts are forbidden. This was a tremendous blow to railroad workers. They were not even granted a union shop, promised at some stages of the negotiations. On the contrary, W. W. Atterbury, the hated president of the Pennsylvania, had drafted in clauses under which company unions might be sanctioned by the courts. Not until the Railway Labor Act was amended in 1934 were company unions effectively outlawed. It was not until 1947 that the AFL began to get union recognition in the Pennsylvania Railroad's shops.

The 1926 law provided that months of mediation, arbitration, and special boards would follow every decision by railroad unions to fight for major contract gains. These mediation and arbitration boards were stacked against labor. During their meetings the old contracts remain in effect. This gives the railroads and the press time to mount propaganda campaigns against the workers. Under the barrage of propaganda and elapsed time, the issues can seem to lose their immediacy. "Emergency boards," which have been set up countless times since 1925, lent all the more authority to the position of the companies and the government.

The Needs of Capital

The decline of railroads stretches across most of the past five decades. A big spurt in the demand for rail transportation during World War II and in the popularity of railroad passenger service immediately following the war temporarily concealed a seemingly inexorable process. In 1930—at the peak—there were 430,000 miles of track being operated in the United States. This had grown from 200,000 miles in 1890. By 1975 it had fallen back to 348,000 miles.

From the beginning of the Depression to today, nearly 100,000 miles of freight and passenger railroad have been eliminated. There have been continual railroad bankruptcies, including all of the biggest eastern lines and an increasing number of midwestern lines. To understand the causes we must take a closer look at the profit needs of railroad capital.

Because they are under private ownership, the railroads in the United States subordinate all other matters to the accumulation of profits. Yet, for reasons we will later indicate, the potential profitability of the railroads is limited, especially compared to such a profitable industry as, for example, oil.

The result is that investment in the railroad industry is curtailed, although the railroads remain a vital necessity. Precisely because they are a social necessity, the owners can continue to extract payment for their use. The railroads continue to generate about $500 million a year in dividends. But all of this is within a context of restricted investment and the continued erosion of whole sectors of the industry. To sort out the causes of this contradictory state of affairs let's begin with a brief overview of the past.

The untrammeled rule of the railroads came to an end in the decade before World War I. Modern capitalist society must, in its own interests, regulate the railroads. If the railroad companies were allowed to set freight rates at will, they would devour many other businesses and most of agriculture. Frank Norris's 1901 novel *Octopus,* for example, vividly described the ruination of California ranchers by the Southern Pacific in the 1890s.

The rule of the railroads produced a massive outburst of antimonopoly sentiment across the nation. Railroads demanded ever-higher shipping rates, wiping out the farmers and small businesses that couldn't afford to pay. The fact that the railroads offered freight discounts to their biggest customers—the Appalachian coal and oil trusts, Pittsburgh steel, and later the auto companies of Detroit— all the more favored these monopolies against their less powerful competitors. Railroad rate regulation emerged as a necessary brake on vested interests which would otherwise destroy much of the economy and did leave whole farming areas and even cities in waste.

There is another less obvious side to this problem. If unlimited freight-rate hikes threatened to destroy almost everybody else, freight-rate wars between the railroads threatened to destroy the railroads themselves. Monopoly profits cannot withstand unlimited price cutting. The strongest capitalists organize monopolies in order to prevent, to the degree possible, price competition.

Owning and controlling large chunks of Eastern railroads enabled the banking house of J. P. Morgan to impose a rate-war treaty on the railroad system and consequently to preserve higher freight rates. But this behind-the-scenes monopoly price fixing was "illegal." It would require the later formation of the Interstate Commerce Commission (ICC) to legalize it.

The ICC performed dual functions. On one side, it would act to prevent the railroads from squeezing other capitalists out; but on the other side, the ICC functioned to prevent the railroads from squeezing themselves out, that is, it protected monopoly profits on the railroads.

The ICC was formed in 1887, the year before the first railroad labor arbitration act was passed. The commission began to get the power to set rates on the eve of World War I. By then J. P. Morgan, Sr., and Southern Pacific's E. H. Harriman were dead. Even the California legislature worked up the courage to lop a few tentacles off Harriman's octopus.

We learned earlier that the Railway Labor Act represents

a compromise in the class struggle between the owners of railroads and railroad workers—with the edge clearly going to the owners. The ICC represents a compromise within the ruling class itself. Limits had to be placed on the power of the railroad monopolies to raise rates at will. From the standpoint of the profit demands of the capital invested in railroads this is not a completely satisfactory compromise. Capital flows to the arenas of highest potential profit. The most profitable industries are those where, for a given period of time, there are few limits on the raising of prices.

We already mentioned the U.S. oil industry. With President Carter's elimination of controls on domestic crude and retail prices, there has been a sharp escalation of prices and profits at all levels and a massive increase of investment in the oil industry.

Situations short of this can discourage capitalist investment. But this also makes the ICC-regulated private ownership of the railroads completely unsatisfactory from a social standpoint. The private owners of the railroads refuse, in the face of limited potential profitability, to make the massive investment society needs to upgrade railroad freight and passenger service.

When the rulers of American industry realized they could not allow railroads to raise rates at will they nevertheless refused to take the needed next step of dismantling private ownership and placing the railroads at the disposal of society. They locked this industry in the hands of its stock- and bondholders.

At the same time, two other sectors of U.S. industry displaced the railroads as the main generators of profits: oil, which began large-scale production in the 1870s, and auto, which became a major industry after the First World War.

Statistics for 1977 vividly illustrate the change. In that year General Motors had greater assets than the eight biggest railroads combined (Union Pacific, Burlington Northern, Southern Pacific, Santa Fe Industries, Seaboard Coastline, Missouri Pacific, Chessie System, and Norfolk and Western). The total assets of these eight railroads were $25.6 billion. GM's assets were $26.7 billion. Exxon, the biggest oil company, had the staggering asset total of $38.4 billion.

Profit levels tell the same story. In 1977 the combined profits of the eight biggest railroads were $985 million; Exxon's profits were $2.4 billion and General Motors's profits were $3.3 billion—six times as much as the eight biggest railroads. Together GM and Ford employ more workers in America than all the railroads combined.

The growth of the auto, trucking, and oil industries has been assisted by massive government investment in the highways and the parallel elimination of railroad service, particularly in the cities. It is well documented that General Motors, Firestone Tire, and Standard Oil of California conspired to eliminate trolley systems in major cities, such as Los Angeles.

"By 1949," according to a Senate subcommittee, "General Motors had been involved in the replacement of more than 100 electric transit systems with GM buses in 45 cities including New York, Philadelphia, Baltimore, St. Louis, Oakland, Salt Lake City, and Los Angeles."

In New York City today, a project to build a new superhighway system, the "Westway," down the west side of Manhattan is under dispute. Comparing this project with PATH, the municipal railroad system that links New Jersey and New York, PATH Vice-president Louis Gambaccini declared, "The total capital investment over fifteen years by the Port Authority of New York and New Jersey in its rail subsidy is $250 million—*equivalent to but one mile of New York City's proposed Westway.*"

The end result of this whole historical process favoring motor vehicles has been a shift of freight carrying away from the railroads to trucking. (See graph next page.)

In the same period the railroads all but discontinued passenger service, pointing to increased auto usage as a justification. But in *To Hell in a Day Coach*, Peter Lyon observes, "Passenger service, to most railroad men, is a nuisance, an irritation, a running sore. It interferes with the potentially lucrative business of carrying freight. Freight is infinitely superior to passengers. Freight, since it is usually inanimate and invariably inarticulate, cannot complain about delays, stupidities, inconveniences, impudences of petty officials, discomforts and shabbiness of railroad cars, filth, squalor of public facilities, breakdowns, derailments, wrecks—in short, the ordinary, day-to-day

TRUCKS GAIN ON TRAINS (Over Three Decades)

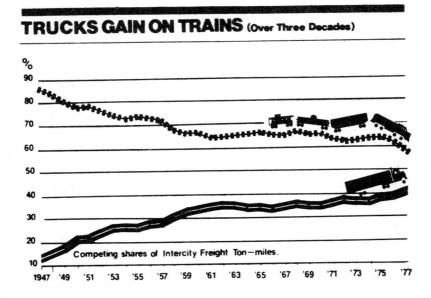

Competing shares of Intercity Freight Ton—miles.

routine of the railroads. . . . Beginning as early as 1920, the presidents of the biggest railroads . . . began to prune passenger trains from their schedules by the dozens and by the hundreds."

The problem of the long-term decline of profit rates on the railroads is well known to the managers of the railroad companies. They use it to excuse the shoddy conditions and lack of new investment which permeate most of American railroading. Yet there is little evidence railroad management grasps the most basic cause of its profit problems. All too often the decline of railroad profitability is simply blamed on rate regulation and government subsidization of the auto industry through highway building. There are more basic reasons for the decline of railroad profitability.

Karl Marx showed that only living labor in the production process creates the new value from which capitalist profits derive. The workers add more value to the products they create than they receive in wages to buy the necessities of life for themselves and their families. The difference—*surplus* value—is pocketed by the capitalists.

Every production process also uses up raw materials,

tools, and semifinished goods. These gained their value when they were produced because of the labor expended on them (mining the coal, machining the tools, etc.). The value of the raw materials used up and machinery partly worn out in the production of new commodities is *transferred* to these commodities in the course of production. The raw materials, machinery, and so on used up in production produce no *new* value; only living labor does that.

What does this mean on the railroads? Railroads do not produce a physical commodity. But the labor of railroad workers is transporting raw materials to factories where they can be processed, or in transporting finished goods to markets where they can be sold, *adds* new value to those commodities. And that is the basic source of the railroad companies' profits: surplus value produced by the labor of railroad workers.

From the outset, however, the railroads' investment in labor power has been relatively small compared to the huge total capital investment required. Thousands of miles of track have to be laid, requiring bridges, tunnels, cuttings, and embankments. Yards, towers, and terminals have to be constructed and the rolling stock purchased. As technology advances, fewer and fewer railroad workers are employed to operate more and more expensive equipment.

It is this disproportionality that is the "secret" of the long-term decline of profitability in railroad investment. The vast capital expenses of the railroads—which do not give rise to profits—came to be an ever-greater burden on the value-producing capacity of the companies.

From the beginning, the companies had to undertake a massive flotation of bonds—that is, borrow money—to build and operate the railroads. (They also looted hundreds of millions from the taxpayers, as we have seen, through various government giveaways and swindles.) The ever-accumulating debt of the railroads meant they had to lay out an increasing portion of their income simply to pay the interest. But this paper claim to values always threatened to overstretch the value-creating capacity of the railroad labor force itself.

If we go back to the comparison between the eight biggest railroads and General Motors made earlier in this chapter, we find that the total debt of these railroads in

1977 was $7.8 billion. This compared to GM's debt of $1.2 billion. Thus, in 1977, these eight railroads had 6.5 times the debt but less than a third of the profits of General Motors. The swollen debt and shrunken profit margin are intimately related. The huge railroad debt is both a cause and an effect of the long-term declining profitability of the railroads.

Here is how these investments operated. At the beginning of each investment cycle—looking again at the latter part of the nineteenth and early twentieth centuries, when the railroads were expanding west—railroad investment seemed to offer unlimited possibilities. There was a great need for railroads in each new area settled. The railroad companies could sharply increase their rates, particularly if they monopolized a given region for a period of time. And they were given vast tracts of land by the government, eliminating this capital expense.

These profitable conditions paved the way for consistent "overbuilding" of railroads. Flush with profits, a railroad company might soon decide to break into the territory of competitors—and float more stocks and bonds on the way.

This whole process inevitably leads to crisis. At a certain moment a given region is saturated with "too many" competing lines. In the course of the boom, freight rates have been jacked up far beyond the actual value added to the commodities being transported. But now the reality—that not enough value is being created to pay off the debts on which the expansion was based—asserts itself with a vengeance. Drastic price slashing then sets in and profits collapse. Railroad stock and bond prices collapse as well. This precipitated the great financial panics of 1873, 1893, and 1907 and the general economic depressions that followed the first two crashes.

This enormously destructive boom-and-bust cycle was capitalism's mechanism for bringing the amount of capital invested in the railroads back into line with the profits the industry's work force could generate. This mechanism worked in two ways. First, economic depression and mass unemployment allowed the slashing of wages, so that more profit could be squeezed out of each worker. Second, huge amounts of railroad capital were simply destroyed through bankruptcy, abandonment of lines, junking of rolling stock, and so on.

A similar process took place in the 1920s and 1930s. In the depression of the 1930s the railroads slumped to their most unprofitable levels ever. By this time, however, with the rise of the oil, auto, and trucking industries, railroading was no longer as central in the American economy. And, as outlined earlier in this chapter, regulation was well underway, interrupting the "normal" shaking-out process of the capitalist profit system. Railroad stock- and bondholders were assured that dividends and interest would continue to flow, but profit levels were simply not adequate to generate the investment needed to maintain and improve the railroads. Some of the worst social disruptions caused by private ownership of the railroads were temporarily alleviated—only to reappear in acute form decades later.

One result is the continuing bankruptcy of railroad lines. Railroad lawyers became experts on using bankruptcy to the advantage of investors. They virtually invented the rules.

According to economic historian August Bolino, there were 80 railroads in bankruptcy in 1876; 192 in 1894; 94 in 1916; and 108 in 1939, on the eve of World War II. Whole sections of the federal government are devoted exclusively to railroad bankruptcies and their consequences.

Which railroad lines to close down without hurting local business too much, which lines to merge into other corporations without seeming to be too much the benefactors of these corporations, how to reimburse the owners of defunct railroads without attracting too much attention—these questions have cudgeled the minds of American corporate lawyers, judges, and politicians since the 1840s.

The crisis wracking the railroads today is the *only way capitalism has to offer* for putting rail transportation on a sound—meaning profitable—basis. Bankruptcies serve to eliminate thousands of miles of track, scrap millions of dollars worth of useful equipment, and centralize operations in the hands of a few profitable companies. Meanwhile thousands of jobs are wiped out and the labor of those remaining is intensified so that the companies can squeeze more profits out of each worker.

Separated from private ownership, the railroads would have none of these problems. Viewed socially, the greater the investment, the cleaner, faster, safer, and more accessible the railroads, the better. If this reduces the labor time necessary, so much the better, because it can lead to a shorter workweek and free up labor for use elsewhere in society. But it also might require many more railroad workers, especially in passenger service. These questions ought to be answered on the basis of the needs of society, not of profits.

Earlier I placed quotation marks around the words "overbuilding" and "too many" because the railroads were overproduced only from the standpoint of private profits. Small communities need and want railroad branch lines, the elimination of which often threatens the very lifeblood of these towns. Only because the branch lines brought railroad companies face to face with *competing companies*, perhaps forcing them to cut rates, were these branch lines a problem for the capitalists. Especially if at some point down the line the same capitalists found they could no longer "justify" the capital costs of maintaining these branch lines. The small communities do not produce sufficient revenues.

Eliminating the profit drive as the criterion for operating the railroads would eliminate the necessity of this kind of closing. A railroad system nationalized and operated for the benefit of the public, could seek to reduce rates and possibly make passenger travel free. It could explore the many ways in which a tremendous new investment in railroads would improve public transportation throughout the United States.

Who Owns the Railroads?

In 1937 Ferdinand Lundberg wrote *America's Sixty Families*, a comprehensive study of the American ruling class. Lundberg proved beyond question that a tiny number of families owned and controlled the biggest U.S. corporations as well as the Democratic and Republican parties and the press.

It is interesting to note how important oil, auto, and rail are in the concentration of power of the American ruling class. Lundberg listed the following nine family groupings, in descending order, as the most wealthy out of the "Sixty."

1. Rockefeller   Oil
2. Morgan   Banking, steel, rail
3. Ford   Auto
4. Harkness   Oil
5. Mellon   Aluminum, oil
6. Vanderbilt   Rail
7. Whitney   Oil
8. Standard Oil Group*
9. Du Pont   Chemicals, auto

Lundberg's list already testifies to the rising power of auto and oil—especially oil—in the American ruling class in the 1930s and the relative decline of the railroads. World War II gave this process an enormous impetus. General Motors and Ford converted their plants to produce the

*In the Standard Oil Trust, the dominant family was the Rockefeller family. The next most powerful partners were the Harkness and Whitney families. Lundberg then grouped a third echelon of families in the Standard Oil Trust as the eighth most wealthy sector of the American ruling class. Today this trust includes Exxon, Mobil, and Standard Oil of California.

instruments of war; the Standard Oil trust provided the fuel. Moreover World War II brought the oil trusts one of the most valuable foreign prizes of the war, the oil of Saudi Arabia, which was to be entirely monopolized by U.S. trusts for the subsequent three decades.

It is commonly thought that the "Robber Barons," who admittedly ruled American industry in the nineteenth century, somehow disappeared in the twentieth. Lundberg showed that in the 1930s this was far from the case. And neither is it true today.

The truth is that the American ruling class *conceals its wealth*. Ownership of stocks and bonds is secret. Not even the U.S. government itself has been able to pry open the secret books of corporations and banks to see who owns them.

It happens that in the 1970s one of the most far-reaching studies of corporate ownership in American history was undertaken by the late Senator Lee Metcalf, but Metcalf's results have not gotten the attention they deserve.

Metcalf was never able to locate *who* the actual owners of corporations are, but he was able to find out *where* their shares are held and *how many* shares are held.

He found that the overwhelming majority of the controlling shares of the biggest U.S. corporations are held in trust funds of the major eastern banks. In many cases the banks themselves *vote* these stocks and consequently directly do control the corporations even though banks don't own the stocks.

Metcalf listed the controlling interests in the 124 largest U.S. corporations in a report entitled *Voting Rights in Major Corporations*, released by the Senate Committee on Governmental Affairs in January 1978.

This showed that the Morgan Guaranty Trust, the direct descendant of J. P. Morgan and Company, held significant interests in eight of the ten largest U.S. railroads—and that it was the biggest shareholder in four of these railroads.

Of the eight largest U.S. railroads Metcalf covered, in which Morgan Guaranty held shares, it ranked as follows:

Burlington Northern	(1st)
Chessie System	(17th)
Norfolk & Western	(1st)

Santa Fe	(1st)
Seaboard Coastline	(10th)
Southern Pacific	(5th)
Southern Railway	(1st)
Union Pacific	(13th)

If anything, the banks are more central in the control of railroads today than they were in J. P. Morgan's time. This is partially the result of processes we discussed in the previous chapter. The manipulation of railroads by a single or several capitalists as investment vehicles to reap big immediate gains faded with the decline of railroad profit rates. The big money was in oil and auto, later in electronics and aerospace (although a fast buck can be made speculating on railroad bankruptcies, as we will see in the next chapters).

But this did not mean that the railroads ceased to generate profits for their ruling-class owners. On the contrary the need for railroads by agriculture and a whole series of major industries, along with Interstate Commerce Commission protection, meant that the railroads would continue to operate. Dividends on stocks and interest on bonds would continue to flow to the owners of the companies. Far from valueless, the paper securities would continue to pump high annual yields to their owners decade after decade.

Federal law, however, prevents banks from owning common stock in corporations, since it is through stock ownership that the voting control of corporations is exercised. Granting the banks unlimited privilege in this regard would have destroyed any other basis of corporate power in this country. But the banks do act as repositories of the common stock in trust funds which the banks manage, sending off the dividends to the owners of these funds. And often the banks are given the power to vote the stocks of these trust funds, thereby establishing an indirect banking control of the corporations.

In the typical situation, consequently, a railroad's common stock will be held in bank trust funds for private owners; in other financial institutions like holding companies, also for the benefit of private owners; and in life insurance companies and pension funds. The bonds will be held directly by the banks, insurance companies, and some private individuals. According to Senator Metcalf's study, as an example, Morgan Guaranty Trust held 4.03 percent of the voting stock of Burlington Northern in 1976. The thirty top holders of this company's common stock as shown in Metcalf's study are reproduced below.

On this list we find five of the ten largest U.S. banks— Bank America, Citibank, Chase Manhattan, J. P. Morgan, and Bankers Trust; two of the largest life insurance companies—Equitable and Bankers Life; a smattering of pension funds; and a number of holding companies whose obscure names have meaning only to Wall Street insiders.

Much publicity has recently been given to pension funds and to the idea that they are taking over stock ownership. This is largely antiunion propaganda. The reality, as Metcalf's report disclosed, is that pension funds are normally voted by the banks, which act as trustees. In terms of voting authority in corporations, Metcalf found that pension funds had only 4.4 percent of voting rights. The results of Metcalf's study on the voting authority in major U.S. corporations are shown in the pie chart on page 64.

This pie chart shows that 50.3 percent of common stock voting authority is held directly by Americans, sometimes through their brokers or other types of investment companies where the investment companies do not own the stock, but merely manage it. In the second largest category, 25.2 percent of the stock is held in bank trust funds, where the banks have been given voting power of 15.6 percent and partial voting power over the remaining 9.6 percent. To begin with, then, 75.6 percent of the shares of stock in U.S. corporations are directly owned by private individuals. Six and a half percent are owned by foreign investors.

The remaining shares are held in a variety of ways. Foundations and educational endowments hold 4 percent. Here the trustees of these institutions vote the stock. Insurance companies and investment companies (where the companies own the stock) hold 9.6 percent. In these cases the owners of these companies profit from the stocks and they are voted by the directors of the companies. In the case of pension funds, the stocks are voted by the pension fund trustees.

This close examination of the situation shows that the overwhelming majority of stocks in corporations are held

Burlington Northern, Inc.

PRINCIPAL STOCKHOLDERS	MANAGED HOLDINGS		
	Voting Power		Total Managed Holdings
	Number of Votes	Percent Total Votes	
1. Morgan Guaranty Trust Co Of NY	514.600	4.03	622.800
Davidson, Daniel P* Dir			
2. Pacific Power & Light Co	344.850	2.70	344.850
Decker Coal Co			
Westana Corp (344850)			
3. Lord Abbett & Co	343.200	2.68	343.200
Affiliated Fund (343200)			
4. TIAA-CREF	181.200	1.42	181.200
College Retirement Equities Fund (181200)			
5. Citibank NA	118.291	.92	163.485
6. Equitable Life Assurance Society Of The US	100.000	.78	100.000
Hendrickson, Robert M* Dir			
7. Continental Investment Corp	100.000	.78	100.000
Waddell & Reed Inc			
United Accumulative Fund (100000)			
8. Minnesota State Board Of Investment	94.700	.74	94.700
9. Washington National Corp	70.000	.54	70.000
Anchor Corp			
Anchor Growth Fund (70000)			
10. USLIFE Corp	62.800	.49	62.800
Sentinel Advisers Inc			
Sentinel Common Stock Fund (62800)			
11. First Wall Street Settlement Corp (NY)	50.701	.39	50.701
12. Adams Express Co	50.000	.39	50.000
13. Oppenheimer & Co	50.000	.39	50.000
Oppenheimer Management Co			
Oppenheimer Fund (50000)			
14. St Paul Companies Inc	47.500	.37	47.500
St Paul Fire And Marine Insur Co (41000)			
Western Life Insur Co (6500)			
15. Bankamerica Corp<	45.655	.35	44.757
16. Bankers Life Co (43100)	43.500	.34	43.500
B.L.C. Equity Management Corp			
B.L.C. Fund Inc (400)			
17. Northwest Bancorporation<	39.387	.30	49.782
Northwestern Natl Bk Minneapolis (49782)			
18. New England Mutual Life Insur Co (2700)	36.700	.28	36.700
Loomis, Sayles & Co Inc			
New England Life Side Fund (34000)			
19. Vance, Sanders & Co Inc	35.000	.27	35.000
Second Fiduciary Exchange Fund (15000)			
Vance, Sanders Special Fund (20000)			
20. United States Trust Co Of NY	33.235	.25	54.232
21. Pittsburgh National Bank	30.759	.24	31.009
22. Penn Mutual Life Insur Co (27500)	29.100	.22	29.100
Penn Mutual Equity Services Inc			
Penn Mutual Equity Fund Inc (1600)			
23. Axe (E W) & Co Inc	25.000	.19	25.000
Axe-Houghton Stock Fund (25000)			
24. Chicago Public School Teachers Pn & Retir Fd	25.000C	.19	25.000C
25. Oregon Public Employees Retirement System	25.000F	.19	25.000F
26. First National Bank Of Minneapolis	9.512	.07	22.130
27. Manufacturers National Bank Of Detroit	4.120	.03	102.420
28. Chase Manhattan Corp<	2.000	.01	58.000
29. Mellon Bank NA	1.444	.01	32.784
30. Bankers Trust Co	-	-	153.000
TOTALS	2.513.254	19.66%	3.088.650

```
TOP  5 SHAREHOLDERS VOTE 11.75% OF THE STOCK.
TOP 10 SHAREHOLDERS VOTE 15.10% OF THE STOCK.
TOP 15 SHAREHOLDERS VOTE 17.00% OF THE STOCK.
TOP 20 SHAREHOLDERS VOTE 18.47% OF THE STOCK.
TOP 25 SHAREHOLDERS VOTE 19.53% OF THE STOCK.
```

Division of Common Stock Voting Authority in U.S. Corporations

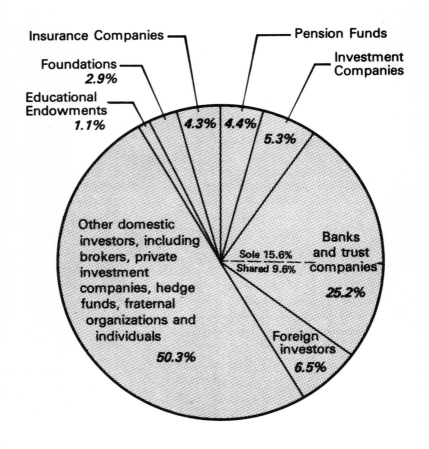

Insurance Companies

Pension Funds

Foundations
2.9%

Investment
Companies

Educational
Endowments
1.1%

4.3% **4.4%**

5.3%

Other domestic
investors, including
brokers, private
investment
companies, hedge
funds, fraternal
organizations and
individuals
50.3%

Sole 15.6%
Shared 9.6%

Banks
and trust
companies
25.2%

Foreign
investors
6.5%

and voted by private individuals. These privately owned corporations include the banks, insurance, and investment companies themselves.

Who are the stock owners? Here the going becomes more murky. The owners of industry do not reveal their names and there are no laws compelling them to do so. On the contrary, the identity of owners is one of the most closely guarded secrets in capitalist America. In nearly a decade of investigation Senator Metcalf was never able to reveal the names of the banks and holding companies where the stocks are held. This did, however, hint at gigantic holdings in some trust funds.

In 1972, according to an earlier report, a secretive account in the Chase Manhattan Bank—not Morgan Guaranty—was the largest holder of railroad shares. In fact this trust fund, with the obscure name of Cudd & Co., was a top shareholder in sixty-two of the biggest U.S. corporations. Metcalf's *Disclosure of Corporate Ownership* was published in 1973. It showed that in 1972, Cudd & Co. was the third largest stockholder in Mobil Oil; Ford Motor, second; Chrysler, seventh; American Telephone & Telegraph, fifth; First National City Bank, fourth. Its holdings in the railroads were:

Penn Central	(19th)
Burlington Northern	(1st)
Norfolk & Western	(2nd)
Chesapeake & Ohio	(11th)
Seaboard Coast Line	(2nd)
Southern Railway	(1st)
Chicago Milwaukee	(5th)
St. Louis-San Francisco	(2nd)
Rio Grande Industries	(4th)
Kansas City Southern	(2nd)

Senator Metcalf's 1978 report on stock voting authority no longer lists the individual trust accounts in each bank, like Cudd & Co., but only the total shares managed in each bank. Further it showed that in 1976 Morgan, not Chase Manhattan, was dominant in such lines as the Burlington Northern and Southern. Were hundred of thousands of railroad securities shifted from one New York bank to the other between 1972 and 1976? Are there complex arrangements whereby shares held in one bank are voted by the

DIVIDENDS IN 1975

Family income level	Percent of the returns in this level*	Percent of this level of income which receives dividends**	Average dividends per return
Under $10,000	53.8%	6.6%	$941
10,000-under 15,000	18.3	8.9	1,231
15,000-under 20,000	12.6	11.7	1,327
20,000-under 25,000	6.8	16.9	1,446
25,000-under 30,000	3.3	25.1	1,949
30,000-under 50,000	3.3	41.0	3,076
50,000-under 100,000	1.0	63.0	7,892
100,000-under 200,000	0.2	77.6	22,305
200,000-under 500,000	0.03	86.2	70,660
500,000-under 1,000,000	0.003	89.8	225,037
1,000,000 and over	0.001	93.1	720,786

*Based on the number of returns, rather than the population. Remember that several members of a given family may be included in a single tax return. But that is true whatever the income level so that this breakdown by returns gives a pretty accurate picture of the overall breakdown of dividend income in American society.
**That is, the percentage of returns at this income level showing dividend income.

other? Who owns the shares in a gigantic trust account like Cudd & Co.?

Not long after Metcalf's 1973 report, Nelson Rockefeller became vice-president and a Senate committee purported to investigate his wealth. Since David Rockefeller was then the chairman of Chase Manhattan Bank it occurred to me that the senators ought to ask Nelson Rockefeller who owns Cudd & Co., and I suggested this in a front-page article in New York's *Village Voice* printed the week of the hearings.

The Senators were apparently too polite to trouble Rockefeller with such a question, although Rockefeller did attack the *Voice* as a "scurrilous rag" during the hearings. Rockefeller took office without anyone penetrating the inner sanctum of industrial, bank, and railroad securities that the Rockefeller family owns.

Although the names of the owners of American corporations are hidden, it is nevertheless possible to get some inkling of the distribution of stock ownership in this country from tax reports compiled by the Internal Revenue Service. The figures for 1975 were published by the IRS in 1978.

These showed that of all the individuals or families in America filing income tax returns, only 11 percent of the returns showed any dividends at all. And this number of shareholders is actually declining in this country because of the increasingly severe jolts on the stock exchange, which smaller holders cannot weather. Among the 11 percent who did receive dividend income in 1975, moreover, there was a wide variety in the amounts received and corresponding number of shares held.

The lower the income level, the lower the number of shares held, and the smaller the proportion of people in this income level who own any shares. Some families have inherited or saved up over a lifetime several hundred shares of one or another blue-chip stock. But most families have no stocks. *Eighty-nine percent* of American families live in this situation—they mostly have no stocks, or if they have them, they are small holdings.

Stockholdings increase in the income bracket of $25,000 to $100,000, especially in the higher ranges. Managers and wealthy professionals will possibly hold several thousand shares of stock in five or ten companies. The income here can be up to around $8,000 a year in dividends, which is large but not enough to live on and nowhere near the holdings of the ruling class itself. This intermediate bracket is roughly *ten percent* of the population.

We are then left with actually *less than one percent of the population*, people whose annual incomes are over $100,000 a year, who receive substantial dividend income. Within this, a still smaller fraction of the population, two ten-thousandths of one percent, a little over one thousand people in all, averaged over $700,000 a year in dividend income in 1975! This is the ruling class. It also receives income from bonds, capital gains, real estate, etc. (A detailed breakdown of the dividend income is shown in the table.)

The myth that multitudes of people own stock and consequently that there is no ruling class in this country is largely derived from not realizing the qualitative difference between holding a few shares and owning a controlling interest. In 1972 the shares of Burlington Northern sold for about $45. If you and I pooled resources we might be able to purchase ten shares—$450; we would certainly have balked at one hundred shares—$4,500. And anything more than that would have been beyond imagining. But in 1972 the Rockefeller depository Cudd & Co. held 821,901 shares worth $36,985,770. These are the holdings that represent controlling interests. They are accessible to only a tiny fraction of the population.

*   *   *

In the yards, railroad workers see bank decals on the locomotives. These decals signify a century-long evolution of the U.S. railroad industry. The railroad companies themselves do not own all of the rolling stock; they must lease it from banks and other distant owners. Very likely the same banks hold and manage the stocks and bonds of the railroad companies, the private ownership of which is key to the mismanagement of the railroads today.

Part of Biltmore House, George Vanderbilt's country house near Asheville, North Carolina. Built 1890-95, it has 250 rooms, including laundries, stables, storerooms, bowling alleys, an indoor pool, and a 72- by 42-foot banquet hall.

Bankruptcies

Throughout the eastern United States, railroads are bankrupt.

This includes the Penn Central, once the biggest of all railroads; Conrail, which is the biggest freight carrier in the United States today; the Boston and Maine; Central of New Jersey; Erie Lackawanna; Lehigh Valley; and Reading.

Railroad bankruptcies are spreading to the Midwest. The Rock Island has been bankrupt since 1973; the Milwaukee Road lunged into bankruptcy in 1977.

These bankruptcies are being used as a major propaganda weapon in the national profit drive of the railroad trusts. The companies implore workers to sacrifice in order to keep each individual employer from going under.

Speedup, unsafe working and traveling conditions, reduced crews, and lower wage increases are justified in the name of "keeping the railroads alive."

Railroads that earn profit on their operations and are not faced with financial problems—that is, the majority of American railroads—of course argue that their employees must make similar sacrifices. If they don't, the bosses say, it will be only a matter of time before the profit-making companies also go into receivership. Then even more layoffs will follow.

The public is being told the same thing, and the bankruptcy-of-the-railroads argument is being used to virtually eliminate long-distance passenger service in this country.

In April 1978 the Milwaukee Road obtained a work-rule settlement with the United Transportation Union giving the company the right to operate systemwide, road and yard, with one-and-one train crews—one conductor and one brakeman, or one foreman and one helper. This reduces the total operating crews, which also include the engineer, from four to three.

Later in the year a Milwaukee Road-type settlement was forced through in Conrail. Other railroads are trying to make it the model for the industry.

The rail union bureaucracies are following suit, warning workers that things will get even worse if they don't make this concession.

In fighting back against this attack on jobs, it is first of all important to underline that most railroads in the country do make profits.

The industry magazine *Railway Age* noted in its January 9, 1978, issue that "roughly 75% of the industry [is] in reasonably good health. The railroads in the South, the railroads in the West, and many of them that operate in the middle western part of the country have main lines that are in good to excellent shape." By excellent shape they mean high profits—they are not talking about the quality of track, usefulness and safety for the public, or the working conditions of railroad workers.

The lines actually in bankruptcy are Conrail, accounting for 12-13 percent of U.S. railroad mileage, and the other companies listed, counting for another 12-13 percent.

These companies reached the point—by varying degrees in each case—where it is no longer possible to finance the enormous debt loads they accumulated over decades and at the same time to continue operations on their previous scale.

Similar to the financial crisis of many cities, the question in railroad bankruptcies is what can the given railroad do to go on paying off its debts? Or, to turn the question around, what must the ruling class do so that the banks, insurance companies, and other financial institutions that have purchased railroad bonds can continue to receive the interest on the bonds that are not due and be confident of refinancing the bonds that are due?

Railroads that cannot meet these payments are put into receivership; that is, they are managed by the ruling class for a shorter or longer period through its courts. The justices' sole task is to restore the line to solvency—to get it back onto the track of paying off its bondholders.

A rail worker for the Northwestern in Chicago told me, "We see every day the amount of money that is wasted, the neglected plant and equipment. Just a bolt needs to be tightened here. Routine management could save this company a lot of money, especially when you see the cost of these derailments." Similar thoughts are expressed by many railroad workers: "Why don't they just run this damned thing right?"

But in all too many cases railroad management is not concerned with the day-to-day operations of the railroads. They may even be deliberately running the particular railroad into the ground, as many Milwaukee Road workers told me. The managers' central preoccupation is to cull the last cent possible out of an industry that throughout the East and Midwest is on the decline. And the entire population in the area is suffering from this.

Among the main victims of this decline are rail workers themselves. The essence of the stepped-up national attack on railroad workers is to make them bear the brunt of the financial problems of the weaker companies. This will prolong the profitability of the weaker railroads and all the more increase the profitability of the big southern and western carriers.

The railroad directors have a very clear program in mind for rail labor. They want to drastically reduce the number of jobs in order to get more work out of fewer workers.

Railroad management is not concerned with improving working conditions, and they are not interested in public safety or convenience. On the contrary, they want to get the most mileage out of the old and frequently dangerous equipment they already have.

The collapse of the Penn Central in 1970 illustrated aspects of this process. After a century of wasteful competition between them, the two biggest eastern railroads, the New York Central and the Pennsylvania, merged in 1968.

But the managers of the merged line had little interest in investing in the railroad itself, either to improve its notoriously rotten passenger service or to reach out to new freight customers.

Instead they poured money into more profitable ventures elsewhere. The Penn Central already stood as the largest real-estate holder in the East. In New York alone it owned the Grand Central Terminal, Pan Am Building, Biltmore, Barclay, and Waldorf-Astoria hotels, and the ITT, Manufacturers Hanover Trust, and Chemical Bank-New York Trust buildings, among others.

Now it picked up such properties as the Great Southwest

Corporation, which runs the Six Flags amusement parks and has widespread real-estate interests; and the Buckeye Pipeline Company, which delivers fuel oil from Indiana to the Northeast.

While this was happening, a core of inside owners carried out a con similar to the Credit Mobilier scheme of the previous century. A small, closely held company called Penphil bought real estate cheaply and sold it at high profits to the Penn Central.

Involved in this apparently everyday operation of finance capital were David Bevan, Penphil's president, who was the head of the finance committee of the Pennsylvania Railroad; General Charles Hodge, a former partner of Maurice Stans, President Nixon's commerce secretary; and the F. I. Du Pont Company, the securities firm of the Du Pont family. In fact, F. I. Du Pont was the principal investment adviser to the Penn Central. Stans, it was subsequently disclosed, held 37,955 shares of Great Western.

A second scheme was also operating at the same time. The stock of Penn Central had been bid way up on Wall Street on the ballyhoo that the merged company would "put eastern railroading back in business."

Its behind-the-scenes real-estate operations were not widely known. The financial institutions that had purchased the stock cheap and run it way up then began to sell it off at enormous profits, keeping smaller investors in the dark as bankruptcy loomed.

Former Chairman of the House Banking Committee Wright Patman later disclosed that in the two months before the bankruptcy was declared, nine financial institutions quietly dumped 1,861,000 shares of stock. These included the Chase Manhattan Bank (Penn Central President Stuart Saunders was a director of Chase Manhattan); the Morgan Guaranty Trust Company; the Security Pacific National Bank of Los Angeles; and the Allegheny Corporation of Baltimore.

The unravelling of this biggest bankruptcy in American history—which is by no means complete a decade after the event—required creating special courts, setting up the United States Railway Association (USRA), passing three major pieces of congressional legislation, and forming Amtrak and Conrail.

At stake are the vast real-estate and railroad properties of the company, its quantities of rolling stock, and the hundreds of millions of dollars of stocks and bonds—that is, claims to income—that have been floated against these properties.

At the time of bankruptcy, the Penn Central listed no less than thirty different series of outstanding bonds issued at one time or another by it or the corporations it and its predecessors had taken over.

For example, the Penn Central owed on a New York Central and Hudson River Railroad "gold" mortgage bond originally issued at 3.5 percent interest. The face value of this series alone is $75,762,000. It has first lien on 1,145 miles of railroad, lien on two bridges from Albany to East Albany, and a lien on all real estate owned and used in connection with the Grand Central Terminal. (Lien is the claim on the property of a debtor to pay the debt.)

The property concerned here was built decades ago. In fact, this particular bond was originally issued by the Utica and Black River Railroad, one of the lines ultimately subsumed by Vanderbilt's New York Central.

For all these years, bond owners have collected interest on these notes. The central aim of the bankruptcy proceedings is to ensure that the note holders will get the most that can still be extracted now and into the future.

Such paper is far from worthless to finance capitalists. The New York Central and Hudson River "gold" is actively traded in New York bond markets. From a low price of $140 for a $1,000 bond at the time of bankruptcy in 1970, it has risen to a present value of about $670. This is a 478 percent increase—showing that immense profits are made not only from the eventual outcome of the bankruptcy proceeding, but even during it.

During a railroad bankruptcy, the operations do not cease for a minute; federal law requires that the railroads continue to operate through the reorganization process. Only two things change: payment on stocks and bonds is postponed, as the trustees attempt to wrest as much as possible out of the bankrupt line for its stock- and bond-holders; and the top management is taken over by the court-appointed trustees whose job it is to oversee the salvaging operation.

But the bankruptcy of the Penn Central involved such

vast wealth and was so complex that this type of court receivership was coupled with federal intervention. The long-distance passenger lines were put under Amtrak, the National Railroad Passenger Corporation, created by the government in 1970. The freight and short-distance passenger lines were put under Conrail, created by Congress in the Regional Rail Reorganization Act of 1973.

"The corporation shall be a for-profit corporation . . . and shall not be an agency or instrumentality of the federal government," Congress declared concerning Conrail. Unknown to most, Conrail is a *totally privately owned corporation, which is subsidized by the government through tax revenues.*

The United States Railway Association was formed as Conrail's banker in order to act as a buffer between the new corporation and the government. Congress appropriates the funds for the USRA. Though its officers are nominated by the president, it isn't under civil service and its budget is not subject to the normal scrutinies of a federal government department.

In addition to the property received from the Penn Central, Conrail also absorbed portions of five other bankrupt lines: the Central of New Jersey, Lehigh Valley, Lehigh and Hudson River, Erie Lackawanna, and the Reading. Conrail has six directors elected by the USRA and five by trustees of a special stock series issued to the six bankrupt railroads from which Conrail received its properties.

This complicated situation flows from the stubborn refusal of the owners of the eastern railroads to allow their properties to be nationalized. To the contrary, the value of these properties is still under litigation. Conrail obtained the rails and rolling stock of the Penn Central and other bankrupt lines in 1976 at scrap prices. Since Conrail is still operating this equipment, it is argued that these properties actually have a much higher value. Compared to the sale price of about $550 million, lawyers for the old railroads are demanding roughly $7 billion, plus interest, from Conrail.

Through this lawsuit, in other words, the bondholders are demanding a multibillion-dollar tribute for the railroads they themselves ran into bankruptcy. And there are five directors from the bankrupt railroads on Conrail's board to ensure that these ruling-class interests are pursued.

Conrail meanwhile issues its own bonds to finance newly purchased equipment in addition to funds received from USRA. Since Conrail is also a major purchaser of railroad equipment—from concrete ties to diesel locomotives—it acts as a conduit of public tax money back into the private sector in two ways: Conrail funds go to the owners of its equipment bonds, and to the manufacturers of the equipment it purchases.

Meanwhile if Conrail is ever returned to profitability the original railroads lay claim to it through the stock series which are presently held by a special court.

Amtrak is not quite so complex. It is directly funded by Treasury money through the Department of Transportation. The White House appoints its chief officer, who then hires the rest of the staff. As in the case of Conrail a special series of stock establishes its ownership by the old lines. This stock is 2 percent owned by the Grand Trunk Western; 6 percent by the Milwaukee Road; 33.6 percent by the Burlington Northern; and 55.8 percent by the Penn Central.

Thus, what is essentially left of the old Pennsylvania-New York Central system is this: the Penn Central Company, which has the remainder of the real estate, a $7-billion claim to Conrail's property, and technical stock entitlement to Conrail and Amtrak; three quasi-governmental agencies—USRA, Conrail, and Amtrak—which operate the lines on a steadily dwindling scale; a special court where the cross-claims of private property are being adjudicated; the five other bankrupt companies absorbed by Conrail in addition to Penn Central; and the owners of the stocks and bonds of these six bankrupt companies, whose interests are being pressed at every level of the process.

If private property ever demanded a monument to its irrationality, this is surely it. The simple step that would eradicate all of these encumbrances—cancellation of the debt and genuine public ownership—seems not to have ever been considered.

Florida East Coast

While the merger of the New York Central and Pennsylvania ended up with the disastrous mess just described, other postwar mergers served to preserve and enhance the profitability of the lines involved. The Chesapeake & Ohio, Baltimore & Ohio, and Western Maryland combined to form the Chessie System; the Seaboard Coast Line acquired the Louisville and Nashville; Norfolk & Western took over the Nickel Plate. These merged railroads and the old Southern Railway are profitable freight haulers in the South and Middle West. Coal remains one of their biggest businesses: the Chessie owns both coal and timber acreages.

The fifth major railroad in the South—the Florida East Coast (FEC)—is a different story. It merits particular attention. The Florida East Coast is one of the most notorious companies in railroading.

The company weathered fourteen years of strikes between 1963 and 1976. It busted unions. It succeeded in reducing its labor force from 2,541 in 1960 to 765 in 1971—refusing to hire back the workers who had joined in strikes. It eliminated all passenger service.

Bankrupt for thirty years, the FEC earned over $11 million in profits in 1978. Its stock is now among the most highly valued railroad stocks on Wall Street.

The FEC case is worth a close look. It reveals what the railroad companies are really after in their national attack on railroad workers. It offers a glimpse of where the railroad productivity drive can lead if the workers are unable to mount effective opposition.

An article in the May 8, 1978, issue of *Railway Age* heralded the FEC As "Florida's Productivity Showcase."

"On the FEC, as on every well-managed railroad," *Railway Age* declared, "the sacred word in management councils is 'productivity'—and by nearly every known measure, FEC is far ahead of the field."

According to *Railway Age*, the FEC has "by far the lowest labor costs of any major railroad anywhere in the world."

FEC President Winfred Thornton told *Railway Age*, "There's no reason why the industry couldn't do exactly what we have done. . . .

"All we're talking about is maybe 9% of the work force. They would have to change the rules with respect to four things: the eight-hour vs. the 100-mile day; running through terminals; yard and road work separation; and such arbitrary things as starting-time rules."

The fact is that the FEC reduced the work force not by the 9 percent Thornton mentioned but by 70 percent. Leaving that aside, the work-rule changes demanded by Thornton underline what the railroad productivity drive is really all about.

The four work rules mentioned by Thornton are not some incidental fringe benefits for railroad workers. They represent the accomplishments of railroad workers in bitter battles against the arbitrary demands of freight shippers. They are the central gains of these battles.

The 100-mile limit was won in the course of railroad labor struggles over decades. One hundred miles roughly corresponded to what a freight train moved in eight hours. In more congested areas it would be less; on long southern and western stretches, it would be much more. The limit has changed with time and the advance of railroad technology.

The concept is nevertheless vital to railroad workers— that there must be a cut-off point for road service employees. At the mileage limit there are terminals where the road crews are supposed to change.

If for some reason the freight goes the limit in less than eight hours workers are still paid for an eight-hour day. If it takes longer, they get overtime.

The limited distance means that the workers know where they're going to spend the night when they are away from home. It is a place not too far away, and they can regularly return home. They are also guaranteed a full day's pay if they are called in.

The aim of the railroads in attacking these rules is to

make workers completely subservient to the needs of the freight carriers—to return them, indeed, to nineteenth-century working conditions. If this means going 250 miles away from home, whenever and wherever the companies choose, so what?

Terminal run-through is part of the same policy. It means the road crews go through the terminal or division points. This wreaks havoc with the lives of workers who happen to live in those terminal points they used to work out of. Either they no longer get much of a chance to return home at all, or they have to move.

Running through terminals with a single road crew greatly intensifies the labor of that crew and eliminates other jobs. FEC Chairman Ed Ball told *Nation's Business* in July 1977: "In 1960 a freight train running from Jacksonville to Miami required three five-man crews, or a total of 15 men. Today that train is operating for the entire distance with two men."

Getting the road crews to do yard work also means speedup. After the freight has arrived at the terminal, the rail bosses want the road crew to get out and do the switching. It's dangerous because the crews are tired after a day's work. They are unfamiliar with the character of the yard and are often working on strange territory at night.

Starting-up time refers to when the shifts start. Instead of a regular schedule of three eight-hour shifts, the companies want to be able to bring in workers whenever it suits them.

Taking all these changes together, we can see what the companies are driving toward: They want to be able to ship freights only when the cars are full—and that means at any time, day or night.

They do not want to take into consideration the health or safety or welfare of the workers. Their message to railroad labor is, "Work for us when and where we want."

The Florida East Coast's drastic efficiency measures affect shippers as well. According to Robert Sherrill, writing in *Nation* magazine, Miami-area growers complain about the FEC's policy of shipping cars only when full. "If growers don't like it they can send their produce by truck, at twice the rate," says Sherrill.

"Nothing less than a full-car load will be picked up. All

in all, farmers on the Florida tip say that the F.E.C. service is so bad that some of them face ruin."

An article in a later issue of *Railway Age* seemed to carry the process launched by the Florida East Coast all the way through. In a discussion of new concepts in scheduling freight cars it declared that "each car is treated as an 'individual,' with a life cycle of its own. . . ." It stands to reason. If the central aim of the railroads is to treat human workers like freight cars, then the next logical step in this inversion of social relations is to treat freight cars like human beings!

How was it possible for the Florida East Coast to go this far? Part of the explanation concerns the owners of the FEC. This railroad is directly owned by one of the most powerful ruling-class families in America—the Du Ponts of Delaware and Florida.

FEC Chairman Ed Ball's sister Jessie married Alfred Du Pont in the 1920s. Together Ball and Alfred Du Pont built a Florida empire that includes thirty-one banks, more than one million acres of land, the St. Joe Paper Company, two railroads, and countless smaller enterprises. The FEC is owned through St. Joe Paper, which controls 52 percent of FEC stock.

The Du Pont railroad interests aren't limited to Florida. Pierre Du Pont II was a director and member of the finance committee of the Pennsylvania Railroad from the 1930s until he died in the early 1950s.

Ball is a big propagandist for the capitalist private-profit system. In arguing against nationalization of the rails, Ball told *Nation's Business* that "U.S. rail lines, with all their archaic work rules, have an average of only 2.7 employees for every mile of track. In countries where the government owns and operates the lines, the number of employees required per mile of track is considerably greater. For example: 22.1 Germans, 20.9 Englishmen and 12.9 Frenchmen."

There are also, Ball omits to point out, more railroad cars per mile of track in these European countries than in the United States. Nevertheless Ball raises a pointed question: Is railroad efficiency in terms of workers hired per mile really what society needs? Does society want fewer workers and poorer service or more workers and better service?

Is the profit criterion a valid basis for making decisions about railroads?

If all the companies go the route of the FEC—and they want to—the end result will be fewer railroad workers, new troubles for American farmers, and no passenger trains. The jobs will be more tiring and more dangerous. Needed rail services everywhere will deteriorate or be eliminated.

Railroad workers who are fighting against the speedup drive should explain to workers inside and outside of rail what happened with the FEC. It is indeed a model of "free enterprise."

Rail Safety

In Waverly, Tennessee, on February 24, 1978, a tank car filled with liquefied propane exploded in a 500-foot ball of flame. Sixteen persons were killed and forty-five injured—the worst accident in railroad history attributable to the carrying of hazardous cargo.

Two days later, in Youngstown, Florida, a train derailment ruptured a tank car filled with chlorine gas. Eight people were killed and 114 injured.

Only a month earlier, in Pensacola, Florida, a derailment caused the release of deadly anhydrous ammonia gas, killing two people and injuring forty-six.

These three disasters propelled into national publicity—at least momentarily—the growing dangers surrounding the rail shipment of hazardous cargo.

This issue underlines the deteriorating and unsafe conditions of the railroads. It is an issue that draws public attention to the dangerous conditions facing railroad workers. And it is an issue of vital importance to the millions of people who live near railroad tracks.

Track-caused accidents have sharply increased in recent years. According to the Federal Railroad Administration there were 4,260 track-caused accidents in 1976 compared to 1,428 in 1966.

In 1976, 500 of the derailments involved shipments of hazardous substances.

On top of this, the railroads carry most radioactive waste. About 90 percent of spent nuclear fuel is shipped by train. All high-level waste from nuclear weapons production is shipped by rail. And for "security" reasons the railroads themselves are often not told when government shipments contain nuclear waste.

The three rail disasters in early 1978 forced various Washington agencies connected with the railroads to come up with explanations.

On March 15 the Office of Technology Assessment (OTA) issued a report tending to blame the railroad companies. It noted that there were adequate safety laws on the books. They just weren't being followed. "It sometimes costs the railroads less to pay a penalty when a violation has been detected or risk having to pay a penalty, than to stop service," the OTA held.

An extensive hearing was held before the National Transportation Safety Board, April 4-6, 1978. Seldom has the buck been passed more times in three days—even in Washington.

Richard Little, vice-president of the Union Pacific, declared—presumably with a straight face: "There does not appear to be any significant relationship between the financial expenditures on maintenance level of railroad track and the number of really serious derailments, including those involving hazardous materials."

Like many executives before him, Little blamed the workers: "The best way to prevent hazardous material incidents is to adequately train railroad employees," he said.

But the main argument of the railroad is that they don't actually *own* the tank cars. "The Union Pacific owns only a very small number of its own cars," Little stated.

This brought to the stand Jack Kruizenga, president of the Union Tank Car Company of Chicago. Kruizenga came under particular fire because the Federal Railroad Administration (FRA) had passed laws in 1969 ordering safety improvements on tank cars carrying hazardous materials.

These tank cars were supposed to be retrofitted with safer couplers and with head shields to protect the tanks from flying parts of the couplers should these be shattered in a derailment. The FRA had given the companies until 1982 to retrofit the cars. As of the April 1978 hearing, a decade after the law was passed, 25 out of the 23,000 jumbo tank cars that were supposed to be changed actually had the safety improvements.

Kruizenga said that it was difficult for his company to find the cars, which were scattered on rails all over the nation. More important, he said, was the fact that his company does not own the cars. It leases them to the shippers.

This is true. Chemical companies such as Dow and Du Pont lease the tank cars that ship their products from the tank-car companies. And even these chemical companies do not always own the cars.

A large number of the cars and locomotives are owned by outside investors—as any railroad worker knows from bank and other ownership decals that are often riveted on the rolling stock. Outside investors are invited in and given tax shelters to make their investments in the rolling stock.

James King, chairman of the National Transportation Safety Board, remarked at one point in the hearings: "No one's ever really gotten anyone who owned the car." What he meant was the pattern of ownership is so complex as to buffer the owners against damage suits by victims of tank-car explosions.

Government witnesses testified that they did not have the money and personnel to police the railroad companies. With 300,000 miles of track in the United States, there are 286 FRA inspectors. Twenty-two are assigned to hazardous materials.

Union representatives, for the most part, echoed the complaints of the government agencies: there is not enough inspection.

"Every year [our organization] pleads, begs in an effort to have an adequate number of inspectors hired by FRA," said one union official.

These union officials do not appear to recognize the irony of their position. The hearing at which they were pleading is precisely the kind of cover the capitalist government needs for its refusal to interfere with the profits-before-safety ways of the railroad companies.

Over the past century there has been voluminous material printed by the United States government exposing the profit-gouging policies of the railroads. What there haven't been are any moves by the government *against* the profit interests of the railroads.

In marked contrast to the banter of company and government officials at the April hearing was the testimony of some victims of the explosions. Joseph Mooney, administrator of Escambia County, Florida, where there have been a number of derailments, told how a wreck occurred and the FRA wouldn't come down for three days.

This Erie-Lackawanna derailment at Harrod, Ohio, in which tank cars of ammonia and other chemicals exploded, caused the death of a child four blocks away. She was hit by flying debris from the wreck.

"The fourth day we got a call from a local inspector and said, well, that there really wasn't any sense in him coming down at that point since all the wreckage was gone; there is nothing to see, and generally their process was that they accepted the report of the derailment and its causes from industry itself."

Mooney responded to the tank-car company official who claimed he didn't know where his cars were: "Let me suggest, that company knows where to send bills for each one of those cars that are leased."

Jimmy Powers, the mayor of Waverly, Tennessee, where the Louisville & Nashville tragedy took place, declared that "the city lost half of its police force who were either killed or injured, many volunteer firemen. . . . We lost our police chief, our fire chief. Had two firemen killed on the scene. Six businesses were destroyed and five damaged. Five homes were destroyed and five damaged. . . .

"I want to tell you, Gentlemen, when you see thirty of your friends running around burned, their clothes all burned off them and their ears burned and their nose burned altogether and they were friends of yours and you have known them all your life; it is a heck of a sight to see, Gentlemen."

Mayor Shirley Murphy of Belt, Montana, came from another scene of an explosion: "There is not a very good feeling toward the Burlington Northern at this time because of the way they want to settle claims. . . . When they make remarks like they did to Mrs. Stephens's mother that her husband was an older man and his productive years were over with. . . ."

One rail union official who testified raised a question that is worth further consideration. Ed McCullough, vice-president of the Brotherhood of Locomotive Engineers, was explaining how the railroad companies ignore safety norms for locomotives.

He pointed out that there is nothing an engineer can do even when so important an instrument as the speedometer isn't working. There are speed limits depending on the condition of the track and the sharpness of the curves. Following these is obviously a crucial safety question.

But "we operate strictly on the carriers' operating rules," said McCullough. "Engineers can be fired on the spot for not taking out locomotives which they believe to be defective."

This hearing took place during the 1978 national coal strike. McCullough called attention to the fact that railroad workers do not have the same right as coal miners to walk away from unsafe conditions. McCullough indicated that the rail unions were pressing for legislation to win this right.

But the coal miners did not win the right to walk away from hazardous mining conditions through the good will of Congress or regulatory agencies. They won it in union battles. The 1978 strike required going against President Carter's Taft-Hartley injunction as well.

The rail unions could go far in their battle to resist the profit drive of the companies if they took their struggle out of Washington, D.C., to the union ranks, to other unions, and to allies elsewhere in the working class.

Working people throughout the country would support the rail workers if the unions got out the facts. Who is going to oppose the right of an engineer not to take out a defective locomotive? Workers everywhere face the same kind of speedup drive and unsafe working conditions.

But in order to get this support, the rail unions have to go after it. They should take it upon themselves to make every working person in the country aware of the real situation in the railroad industry. No one else is going to do it for them.

The Milwaukee Road
and Rail Productivity

On the evening of June 5, 1978, about 250 railroad workers gathered in Minneapolis in a meeting sponsored by rail union locals to protest the shutdown of the Milwaukee Road. A banner behind the speakers platform declared, "Stop the Milw. Shutdown! Open up the MR Books!" Speaker after speaker testified to how management had deliberately run this railroad into the ground.

James Murphy, a fifty-eight-year-old machinist who repairs locomotive engines in St. Paul, received heavy applause when he declared, "There's been nothing but mismanagement from the top on down and I'm sick of it." Murphy said that when a locomotive needs new parts, the Milwaukee Road's policy is not to go out and buy the parts. Instead other Milwaukee Road locomotives in good working order are "cannibalized" or stripped of their parts. The stripped engines sit in the rail yard while the company continues to make payments to the banks on them, Murphy testified.

R. C. Boughton, a locomotive engineer, told of seeing a perfectly good box car scrapped. He said all that was wrong with it was that a $10 part connected to one of the wheels needed oil.

The Chicago, Milwaukee, St. Paul & Pacific Railroad—the Milwaukee Road—petitioned for bankruptcy in December 1977. Ironically enough this was the Milwaukee Road's *fourth* bankruptcy. The company commenced operations by purchasing the bankrupt Milwaukee & Prairie de Chien Railway in 1863. This was the last of the transcontinental railroads, pushing west from Wisconsin shortly after the turn of the century. It never attracted enough traffic and on March 17, 1925, it filed for bankruptcy. It went bankrupt again in the Depression in 1935, and was under receivership until 1947, when the postwar upswing of the railroads temporarily bailed it out.

In every bankruptcy, the central question for the owners is how to get the most out of the asset value of the company. Securities analysts placed the scrap value of the Milwaukee's "locomotives, tracks, bridges, timber and land" at $832 million according to the July 23, 1978, *Barron's*. The line would undoubtedly be worth a good deal more, certainly more than $1 billion, since the properties that continued to operate would be sold at higher than scrap value.

The stock of the Milwaukee Road had fallen as low as 2 7/8ths per share. After the declaration of bankruptcy it rose as high as 19 7/8ths—a 691 percent increase, which is not a bad take for the owners of a bankrupt company.

This is not an unprecedented phenomenon. The new elements introduced in the Milwaukee Road bankruptcy were the drastic speed-up measures undertaken with the crews and the attempt to drastically reduce or eliminate the compensation to workers who would lose their jobs as a result of the liquidation of the company. The speedup and the threat to eliminate jobs without compensation brought protesters together in Minneapolis, Chicago, and Milwaukee as the bankruptcy proceedings unfolded.

The dangerous character of the jobs in reduced crews and the threat to seniority were emphasized by Bill Peterson, a train-service employee on the Milwaukee Road for most of fifteen years. "They sold it to us as a way of staving off liquidation," Peterson said, "totally ignoring its impact on the jobs."

"According to the agreement, trains with one to seventy cars may be operated with the reduced crews—one conductor and one brakeperson," Peterson said. "Trains from 71 to 120 cars were supposed to keep the three-person crew. But how many trains are less than 70 cars? Very few. The truth of the matter is the company consistently violated this agreement and ran the longer trains with the reduced crews." (I heard the same objection from Conrail workers where the crew-consist reduction had also been pushed through . . . on the grounds of "bankruptcy.")

Peterson continued, "You find yourself alone in the caboose for twelve hours on the road with a train ahead of you over a mile and a half long. It makes it impossible to properly inspect both sides of your train for defects that could cause derailments and so forth. It puts older employees in the position of being required to make emergency repairs. But worst of all, road brakers with twenty or even more years of seniority are being pulled from their regular jobs and forced to work undesirable jobs with long away-from-home layovers, costing them a lot of time and money."

According to *Barron's* a Milwaukee Road lawyer named Leonard Gesas told the judge presiding over the bankruptcy that, "if the entire railroad were to be abandoned, no obligation to labor would exist.

"[Gesas] feels a full abandonment is needed to free the bankrupt Milwaukee from labor's claims. Several of the attorneys for other Milwaukee creditors have taken similar positions. If they're right, abandonment would offer Chicago Milwaukee stockholders the best outcome of all."

This attempt to eliminate compensation is the other new element in the Milwaukee Road bankruptcy. Since the 1930s, railroad workers have enjoyed job protection in the event of mergers. An agreement signed in May 1936 provided that whenever a merger took place between two or more carriers, the displaced employees would receive compensation based on the length of service, payable monthly at the rate of 60 percent of the average monthly compensation of the workers at the time of the merger. This allowance was to continue for five years for employees with fifteen years or more service and for shorter periods for employees with less seniority.

In the postwar mergers this or similar provisions were subscribed to. The Milwaukee Road owners hope to eliminate compensation. And in this way the Milwaukee Road bankruptcy serves as an escalation of the ruling-class attack on railroad workers.

William J. Quinn, chairman of the board of the Milwaukee Road, testified before congressional hearings on the bankruptcy, January 5, 1978. "Quite logically, government could encourage the creation of four 'core-system' railroads in the private sector in the West. These 'core-system' railroads would be fashioned around the existing Southern Pacific, Santa Fe, Union Pacific and Burlington Northern. To these carriers, in a manner prompted by certain incentives, would be added the appropriate marginal and other lines, or at least the essential parts of them. . . .

"No 'core system' railroads, no matter how strong financially, can easily afford the cost of labor protection which this comprehensive plan of rationalization would ultimately create, and which should of course be paid. Here too government should lighten the load on the 'core-system' railroads and on the 'acquired' railroads as well."

And so the chief executive officer of a "marginal" railroad pleaded for government support. The government should pay labor compensation so that the most profitable railroads in the country—the Burlington Northern, Southern Pacific, etc.—can all the more concentrate and centralize western railroading under their command. The fact that Quinn had previously served as president of the Chicago, Burlington & Quincy—one of the roads merged into the Burlington Northern in 1970—adds all the more weight to the Milwaukee Road workers' claim that the line has been deliberately run into the ground so that its bankrupt remains could then be auctioned off cheaply to the more profitable roads.

*   *   *

The drive to speed up production on the railroads is not new. It is deeply rooted in the profit needs of railroad capital. Nor is it unique to the railroads. Everywhere the bosses are attempting to speed up production under more and more hazardous conditions of work. This is a central aspect of the deepening crisis of American capitalism.

The craft divisions in the railroad labor movement and the network of antistrike laws have undoubtedly weakened railroad labor in the face of this productivity drive. Following the depression there have been much greater productivity increases and slower increases of wages on the railroads than in other sectors of basic industry where there are industrial unions. The weekly wages for production workers since 1939 for railroads, coal, and steel are shown in the next table.

WEEKLY WAGES
(Current dollars)

Selected years	Rail	Coal	Steel
1939	$31.90	$22.99	$30.00
1947	55.03	63.75	56.51
1957	94.24	106.00	105.57
1978	343.92	389.50	390.52
Increase	978%	1,594%	1,202%

But these figures do not take into account the inflation which has eroded the purchasing power of the dollar, especially in the last decade. Corrected for inflation the results are even more sobering.

WEEKLY WAGES
(1967 dollars)

Selected years	Rail	Coal	Steel
1939	$76.68	$55.26	$72.11
1978	176.10	199.45	199.96
Increase	130%	261%	177%

The big productivity drive on the railroads came after World War II and it escalated in the 1970s. The following table shows the indexes of production-worker output per labor hour in the same industries since 1947.

PRODUCTIVITY INDEXES
(1967 = 100)

Selected years	Rail	Coal	Steel
1947	36.7	32.1	64.7
1957	53.7	55.6	81.6
1970	110.3	103.8	102.6
1978	155.3	77.5	121.8
Increase	323%	141%	88%

All of these figures must be taken with a grain of salt. They are based on government studies which themselves must rely on company data, and I have had to combine various Bureau of Labor Statistics (BLS) series to compile the tables. Nevertheless the trend is evident. The "aristocracy of the aristocracy" of labor proved itself ill equipped to withstand the speedup on the railroads.

According to an August 1979 BLS report, in 1978 "Railroad productivity was up 12.2 percent, as output grew 3.3 percent and employee hours fell 7.9 percent." These are truly remarkable figures. In the United States economy as a whole, an annual productivity increase above 3 percent is considered somewhat of an accomplishment by the ruling class. The figures for railroad productivity—at four times this level—are the results of intensified speedup and the slashing of crews.

The results of this productivity drive can also be seen in the statistics on ton miles carried (billions of tons carried one mile):

1890		76
1909		219
1924		392
1930		385
1934		270
1939		335
1947		658
1969		773
1979	(estimate)	910

We have already seen the reduction in miles of track operated. Here is the other side of the story. Ever increasing freight haulage by the big and increasingly merged U.S. railroad monopolies.

The perspective of these monopolies seems to be essentially what Milwaukee Road executive Quinn told Congress: Boil the railroads down to a few gigantic systems. If possible do it without compensating the tens of thousands of workers who will lose their jobs. Quinn didn't say the second part of this in so many words, but the way the Milwaukee owners carried out their bankruptcy proceedings showed that this is what they had in mind: The trustees went to a federal court in Chicago to demand a ruling allowing them to phase out the company without labor compensation.

Subsequently the fate of the Milwaukee was juggled by the courts, various congressional committees, the Interstate Commerce Commission, and the Department of Transportation. Each one sought a plan for liquidating the company and paying workers the minimum they could get away with. None had either the workers' interests or those of the farmers and small businesses along the right-of-way in mind.

Quite a different plan emerged from a group of railroad unionists in Minneapolis. In a petition issued September 30, 1979, they said, "The future operation of the Milwaukee Road is in grave danger. Milwaukee Road owners, management, and trustees, with the cooperation of the ICC, the courts, Congress, and the Carter administration, are pressing hard for the liquidation of two-thirds of the Milwaukee system. . . .

"Since it is clearly in the interest of the public to keep the Milwaukee Road running, and since the present owners and managers insist they are incapable of maintaining a fully functioning Milwaukee Road, we call on the Government to take the operation out of the hands of private ownership and management, and nationalize the Milwaukee Road as a public utility, publicly governed by an elected board."

Conclusion

When W. W. Atterbury, the notorious Pennsylvania Railroad executive, died in 1935, railroad workers circulated the following yarn. As Atterbury's coffin was being carried down the aisle of the Episcopal cathedral, the lid suddenly snapped up, the eyes of the corpse glared at the eight pallbearers, and its mouth snarled, "Lay off four of these men." The lid slammed down again.

The joke, recounted by Peter Lyon in *To Hell in a Day Coach*, may have even more meaning today than when it went around the Pennsylvania yards in 1935. There has never been a greater need for railroad transportation. But the railroad companies, placing profit needs above everything else, are cutting back. Thousands of workers are losing jobs. Needed service to farmers and small business is being eliminated. Passenger transportation is being all but abandoned. The jobs that do remain on railroads are getting more dangerous. And the federal government is fronting for the railroad companies in this profit drive.

Through Amtrak and Conrail, Washington stepped in to attempt to help salvage the profits of the bankrupt northeastern railroads. Under the guise of public control, the government in fact carefully preserved the web of private ownership of these railoads. Meanwhile Amtrak and Conrail are in the forefront of the attack on rail workers and the elimination of rail services. Precisely because they have the cover of being quasi-governmental operations, they can more easily come on with the line that *restoring the railroads* is what they are all about.

In fact, what they are all about is *restoring capitalist profits*.

When Conrail was established, dozens of branch lines were closed down and thousands of jobs eliminated.

"Conrail is currently engaged in a labor negotiating

strategy aimed at directly linking employee pay raises with increased productivity," the *Wall Street Journal* reported in 1978. Following this, Conrail was the first railroad after the Milwaukee Road to push a similar crew-cutting pattern through its contract with the United Transportation Union.

Amtrak's threats to slash passenger service all the more lend credence to the myth that "railroad passenger service is old-fashioned, it just doesn't work, people would rather drive than take trains, etc."

Two weeks after Transportation Secretary Brock Adams said he would cut Amtrak service by 43 percent, it was revealed that Amtrak passenger traffic had risen 7.5 percent in 1978. In addition, when the gasoline crisis hit in the spring of 1979 the demand for Amtrak was so great that statistics on passenger service grossly underplayed the real situation. There weren't enough trains to go around. A statistic that did give the picture was the number of *unanswered phone calls* to Amtrak information desks across the country. At five major Amtrak centers in May 1979, this ran to five million!

This disastrous situation ought to be ended. Railroads are a vital national resource that should rightfully belong to all the people. Decisions regarding this resource should be made by the people in free and open discussion—instead of by secretive trusts, whose one and only aim is to keep the dividends flowing.

The railroads in the United States should be nationalized. They should be converted into public utilities where the workers themselves have control over the conditions of work. This does not mean more Amtraks and Conrails. As we have already seen, Amtrak and Conrail are fake nationalizations. Both remain privately owned. Both are operated in the private interests of railroad stock- and bondholders.

What is needed is to take the railroads completely out of the hands of private ownership and run them as public services on a non-profit basis, to benefit the population.

Nationalization can be a big step toward ripping away the cover of "business secrecy," which has served for a century and a half to conceal profiteering and pillage at the public expense by the railroad owners. Once national-ized, the railroads should not be handed over to a gang of government bureaucrats or "regulators," who invariably come from private industry and who are tied in a hundred ways to big business. Instead, the railroads should be managed by an elected public board that works entirely in the open. By insisting that all the meetings of such a board be open to the public, that its books and records be published and available for public inspection, and that its decisions be fully aired and accounted for, working people could keep a close eye on its operations. This would place the working-class majority of society in the best position to fight to safeguard its interests.

Such a railway management board should make all the facts public, not only about railroading but about the availability of coal, oil, and other energy resources which are intimately related to the railroad industry and transportation as a whole. Working people could then become involved in an informed and wide-ranging discussion about transportation and energy needs in the United States.

The best guarantee that the nationalized railroads will be run in the public interest is to entrust control over their day-to-day operations to the rail workers themselves. They must be able to monitor the financial records, assure honesty and accuracy in the reports by management, and supervise the organization of work.

Who knows better than railroad workers what the real situation is, what the capacities of the railroads are, what the present dangers are, and what steps must be taken to improve service? Elected committees of rail workers should have the power to set work schedules and tempo and to make adequate job assignments so that the highest standards of safety and service are met. They must be assured the right to shut down operations that are hazardous to themselves or the public. All legal restrictions on the right of rail workers to organize, bargain collectively, and strike must be abolished.

Instead of the current irrational system of grueling overtime for some while others go jobless, the rail unions should have the power to reduce the workweek for all, with no reduction from the current average weekly take-home pay. Shorter working hours would not only create jobs and give rail workers some time with their families, but also contribute to greater safety. In the past railroad workers led in the struggle for the eight-hour day. Today they could take the leadership again in the struggle for a six-hour day.

The rail unions should have full authority over hiring, firing, and job discipline. This is the way to get rid of the favoritism, racism, and sexist discrimination that rail management now uses to keep workers divided. It would allow the unions to implement affirmative-action programs to assure equality in hiring, promotion, and training for skilled jobs.

The demand to nationalize the railroads is becoming increasingly popular in this country. There is no question about the need to reorganize transportation and energy in the United States. We need a national transportation plan and a national energy plan based on human necessities instead of private profits.

Nationalization of the railroads would end the destructive chase after profits. We have seen that the Interstate Commerce Commission regulates railroad rates. And one of the ways it is supposed to do this is by guaranteeing competition among the railroads. Two lines are maintained across the Northwest (three, including the Milwaukee Road), on the assumption that they will compete with each other to serve customers better.

The presumption is false. The aim of ICC regulation from the outset was to maintain profits for privately-owned railroads within the context of rate regulation. The ICC itself guarantees these profits by steadily *raising* the rates. But the railroads should be run to meet the needs of customers and railroad workers—not for company profits. Merging all of the railroads into a single centrally planned system and eliminating their obligations to parasitic stock- and bondholders would be a significant step in this direction.

Every aspect of the crisis of U.S. railroads highlights the destructive role of the profit drive. This is even noted within the industry.

Railway Age published an article on railroad financing by bond analyst Isabel Benham. Her article concerned the ten biggest U.S. railroads, ranked in order of after-tax profits on assets (Missouri Pacific, Union Pacific, Santa

Fe, Rio Grande, Southern, Norfolk and Western, Seaboard Coast Line, Southern Pacific, Chessie, and Burlington Northern).

She criticizes these companies for paying out so much in dividends to their owners when capital is needed for investment purposes: "As you can see, all 10 companies paid higher dividends in 1977 than in 1973," Benham says. "Several roads have increased their dividends annually in the last five years; two roads have had dividend increases greater than their growth in earnings per share [Chessie and Seaboard Coast Line—D.R.]. . . .

"In 1977 alone, these 10 companies . . . earned over one billion dollars and paid out in cash dividends $435 million, a 43% payout ratio. When it is realized that the industry as a whole anticipates annual capital requirements in the next five years of $3-5 billion and Burlington Northern alone anticipates capital needs of $500 million annually, the need for the railroads to retain every dollar of earnings is self-evident."

But not to those who own and control the railroads for their own enrichment!

The question of rail electrification further underlines the obstacle to social progress created by the private ownership of the railroads. Ecological experts have advanced many arguments for the return of rails to electric energy and the massive reintroduction of electrical railroads in the cities. These would be less polluting and much more convenient for millions of people.

Ironically, rail electrification would also be more economical. It would require lower maintenance costs because each train does not require its own power plant. There would be less possibility of engine failure because many fewer moving parts are involved. The flexible power source (electric power can come from coal, oil, or hydro-energy sources) would reduce energy costs. And these factors would all lead to a longer life expectancy for locomotives, possibly as long as thirty years, compared to the present average of eighteen.

What stands in the way?

For one thing, the financial institutions that control the railroads do not want to spend money on such improvements when their central concern right now is to collect on loans they have already floated. On top of this, there is the opposition of the oil and auto trusts, which helped to dismantle electric railroads in the first place.

The result is a passenger service in and between cities that is old and deteriorating in most cases. Electrical rail services needed in city after city are barely contemplated. Urban mass transportation, which would provide tens of thousands of jobs in construction, is slashed in budget after budget. Nothing short of railroad nationalization and a national transportation plan seems likely to turn this situation around.

Another question that brings together energy and transportation needs is the urgent necessity to shut down all nuclear power plants *now*. Three Mile Island convinced millions of working people that nuclear power is catastrophically dangerous. But the nuclear industry and the government claim there is no alternative—that closing nuclear plants would mean energy shortages, blackouts, and a drastic decline in jobs and living standards. As usual, they are lying.

Many nuclear power plants now in operation have coal generators to back them up. There is abundant coal in this country to serve as an immediate alternative to deadly nuclear power. We are presently using only 1 percent of the known coal reserves.

Coal mining could be made safe if it was put under the control of the miners. Coal burning could be made clean if sufficient funds were allocated for the scrubbers and other necessary environmental protection measures.

Railroad workers have a deep interest in this issue because they have to transport nuclear waste, often in unplacarded cars. It is an issue that the rail unions and the United Mine Workers could immediately agree on. The UMW is already campaigning for a switch to coal.

The coal alternative would provide new jobs in another way. It is hardly a secret that the roadbeds of the old coal hauling companies could not withstand the extra load of freight that such a big increase in coal usage would demand. Following the Waverly disaster described earlier, the *Wall Street Journal* admitted in a front-page article, "So many [Louisville & Nashville] trains have been derailed—hundreds of them in the past two years—that it is becoming apparent that the railroad itself has gone a bit off the track. And at first glance, the L&N's problems seem ironic: After the end of the long coal strike early last spring, the subsidiary of Seaboard Coast Line Industries Inc. should have benefited from the boom in coal haulage. Coal accounts for 48% of the L&N's tonnage. . . .

"But the L&N concedes it hasn't been able to handle the coal boom. . . . Besides derailments, it has been beset with federal fines for safety violations, screaming coal customers, a lawsuit and other woes."

This was before there was any thought of replacing nuclear plants with coal. To rebuild the nation's railroad beds would be still another major source of jobs flowing from a rational approach to transportation and energy. If the restored roadbeds made possible much more rapid passenger trains—that arrive on time!—the job of upgrading would be all the more welcome.

Nationalization of the railroads will meet with plenty of objections from big business. Not least will be the claim that a nationalized rail system would be "too expensive," a drain on tax dollars at a time when taxpayers are already in revolt.

Is American society actually short of the money needed to rehabilitate and expand railroading in this country? The immense military budget can be taken as a standard. The Pentagon projects spending over $150 billion annually on its armed forces and instruments of death. Compared to this the 1979 capital investment plans of the railroads are projected at about $5 billion—one thirtieth the amount.

The experience of Vietnam made clear to millions of Americans what hundreds of millions of people in the rest of the world already knew: that Washington's huge global military apparatus is no defender of freedom and democracy. It is deployed to prop up despots and torturers and repress popular insurgencies. Built up in the name of the "national interest," the Pentagon actually serves the interest of only a tiny segment of society—the owners of the U.S. corporations, who want to exploit the peoples and resources of the world. American working people foot the bill for this war machine with their lives, with their tax dollars, and with paycheck-shrinking inflation caused by the mammoth war budget.

Despite efforts of Democratic and Republican politicians alike to drum up support for even more war spending, there is widespread public sentiment for redirecting these bil-

The Cost of War

This cartoon by John M. Baer first appeared in the railroad union newspaper *Labor* in the early 1920s during its campaign for nationalization of the railroads. The cartoon was reproduced all over the world.

lions to socially useful purposes. Even a fraction of one year's current war spending would serve to totally transform the railroads in a very short time, creating tens of thousands of jobs instead of eliminating them and providing services that are needed by all working people.

Transportation and energy are vital necessities in modern industrial society. Both should be as accessible to working people as air and water. This requires taking them out of the hands of the private owners and putting them at the service of society, under the control of working people.

This perspective can help railroad workers to gain allies. The propaganda of the capitalists is aimed at pitting everyone against railroad workers. The railroads are supposed to be in trouble because of the demands of rail workers. If the rail unions would accept drastic job cuts and "more efficient" working conditions, the railroads would be in better order.

But the real enemy is the profit drive of the railroad trusts. Nor is this productivity drive limited to the rail industry. Everywhere capitalist monopoly is driving to intensify labor, to increase layoffs, and to exact wage concessions from workers.

At first sight the strategies of the energy trusts, awash in profits, seems to have little in common with the aims of the railroads. But the enormous profits of the oil companies stem from their ability to *cut back* oil, natural gas, and gasoline production in this country over a long period. No refineries built on the East Coast in nineteen years; none on the West Coast in seven years; curtailment of oil and natural gas drilling; hoarding of inventories. This slashing of production leads to higher prices. The steel trusts are similarly closing down old plants.

Oil and steel are following paths long ago carved out by the railroads. Private monopoly's answer to profit problems is to cut back production, to hone down to the profitable core, to lay off workers and drive up prices. This is the very opposite of what society needs. We need more and cheaper energy, more and cheaper transportation, and more jobs.

Railroad workers can thus find allies throughout the working class in the fight against job cuts. To do this, they can make the facts about rail working conditions known far and wide. They should get out the facts about the dangers of railroading, the real conditions of the roadbeds, the hazards involved in shipping petrochemicals and other explosive materials.

To the railroad's claims that they can't get by and that they are bankrupt, the railroad workers should respond, "Open up the financial books. Let's see what the real situation is.

"What are the actual organization plans of the railroad trusts? How do they tie in with the plans of the oil trusts? What's the truth behind the bankruptcies? What are the real profits of the railroads? Who owns these companies? Who stands to profit from the spiraling energy prices and the firing of thousands of railroad workers?"

To take the railroad companies out of the hands of their private owners will obviously require a fight. It will require the mobilization of the railroad union ranks and the mobilization of their sisters and brothers throughout the union movement. There can be many allies: farmers, people who live along the rights-of-way and in communities that have much to gain by improved railroad service, and many millions of others who would like to improve living conditions in this country.

Such a fighting perspective is alien to the present top officialdom of the railroad unions. These officials are deeply immersed in capitalist politics and tied up in the courts, and have little remembrance of the titanic battles waged by railroad laborers in earlier times.

They have no feel for the real power of unions, of the union ranks. They rely only on lobbying the government. Some top union officials have taken seats on the phony "public" agencies running Amtrak and Conrail, thus aiding the coverup of this capitalist power grab. In the face of the stepped-up attacks, the union officialdom has helped keep workers in the dark about the extent of the attack and the extent of the fightback.

As the ax fell on the Milwaukee Road, the UTU headquarters in Cleveland said, "Write your congressman." That was it. They offered no plan to inform the membership about what was really happening and mobilize them in the fight to stop it.

But a fighting perspective does make a lot of sense to workers who keep the trains running and who face the mounting attack on working conditions. Many of them are already taking part in local battles to stem this attack.

They are also thinking about the need to transform the union movement. They realize that we need fighting unions and that this requires union democracy. The struggle to gain the right of members to vote on contracts and directly elect the top officials in the UTU is a vital part of the struggle to transform and democratize this union.*

Solidarity is another key to advancing the interests of workers. By respecting the picket lines of the BRAC workers on the Norfolk & Western in their 1978 struggle, workers from other rail unions contributed to the gains won in that strike. The solidarity in the yards in Youngstown and Pittsburgh forced Conrail to step back from its victimization plans. Such solidarity points toward the much-needed step of overcoming the craft divisions among the rail unions.

On top of this, the struggles of railroad workers can win support from people outside the rail unions. It is in the interests of all working people for railroad workers to have the right to strike. Not only railroad workers but everyone who uses, lives near, or crosses railroad tracks has a deep interest in safe working conditions on the railroads, sufficient crew sizes, maintenance of roadbeds, and the elimination of potentially lethal shipments.

There is immense power latent in the American railroad union movement. If railroad workers shut down the railroads, their action immediately affects major sectors of other industries as well. That is why the White House, the U.S. Congress, and federal and state courts, in league with the railroad companies, spent a good deal of the first part of this century encumbering railroad workers with anti-strike laws. That is why virtually every railroad strike brings down an injunction from Washington.

Fighting together with other unions, farmers' organizations, and allies of the workers' movement, rail labor could launch a campaign to reorganize transportation in the public interest.

---

*For details see *A Struggle for Union Democracy—The Story of the Right to Vote Committee in the United Transportation Union*, by Ed Heisler. Available for 75 cents from Pathfinder Press, 410 West Street, New York, N.Y., 10014

Key to unleashing union power will be breaking from the capitalist two-party system. This brief history of the railroads underlines the essential role Washington plays in the profit drive of the railroad companies. From the outset, Republican and Democratic politicians voted the gigantic land giveaways that made private ownership of railroading not only possible but profitable. From the outset, tax breaks from local and state governments, as well as the federal government, have greased the railroads and the palms of their private owners. This is no less so today.

Amtrak and Conrail are subsidized by public tax dollars even though they are actually an elaborate scheme aimed at maintaining the private ownership and private profitability of northeastern railroading. The Democrats and Republicans who voted these agencies into being conceal this hoax from their constituencies.

Washington spearheads the attacks on railroad workers when they attempt to struggle for what is rightfully theirs. Democrats and Republicans alike presided over the formulation and enactment of antilabor laws like the Railway Labor Act.

Workers need their own party, a labor party based on the unions and representing working people and their allies. A labor party is needed which could make the struggle against the railroad and energy trusts a top priority. It could seek the support of working people everywhere, who have an interest in cheap energy and easily accessible mass transportation. It could seek support as well from farmers, who also have everything to gain from cheaper fuel and rail shipping service, and from activists in the environmental and anti–nuclear power movements.

The idea of breaking the control over our lives by giant corporations is being given serious thought by millions of working people. The new moods in the ranks of labor are even finding expression at top levels of the union leadership. Already the AFL-CIO Executive Council and former UTU Chairman Al Chesser have called for nationalizing the oil companies.

Growing numbers of people oppose the disastrous results that flow from putting the profit drive above every other consideration. Some are drawing the logical conclusion that capitalism needs to be replaced by a socialist society based on human needs instead of private profits.

Making the railroads into a real public service has been a wish of many Americans for more than a century, from the inception of railroading. It requires a political struggle to take the railroads out of the hands of private capital and put them at the service of the public. It is long overdue.

Further Reading

Brown, Dee. *Hear that Lonesome Whistle Blow.* New York: Holt, Rinehart and Winston, 1977.

Debs, Eugene V. *Eugene V. Debs Speaks.* Edited by Jean Y. Tussey. New York: Pathfinder Press, 1970.

Foner, Philip S. *The Great Labor Uprising of 1877.* New York: Monad Press, 1977.

Ginger, Ray. *Eugene V. Debs: A Biography.* New York: Collier Books, 1962.

Heisler, Ed. *A Struggle for Union Democracy—The Story of the Right to Vote Committee in the United Transportation Union.* New York: Pathfinder Press, 1976.

Lyon, Peter. *To Hell in a Day Coach: An Exasperated Look at American Railroads.* Philadelphia and New York: J. B. Lippincott, 1968.

Myers, Gustavus. *History of the Great American Fortunes.* New York: Modern Library, 1937.